Exploring Woodland

Yorkshire &
The Northeast

101 beautiful woods to visit

Collins is an imprint of HarperCollins*Publishers* Ltd.
77–85 Fulham Palace Road
London
W6 8JB
The Collins website address is: www. collins.co.uk

10 09 08 07 06 05 04

10 9 8 7 6 5 4 3 2 1

ISBN 0 00 717549 3

First published in 2004
Text © The Woodland Trust 2004
Maps © HarperCollins*Publishers*, except p66 © The Woodland Trust

The copyright in the photographs belongs to the following: Woodland Trust Picture
Library: 6, 8, 15, 25, 26, 29, 33, 34, 39, 42, 44, 55, 56, 65, 68, 84, 88; Simon Miles 4;
National Trust Photographic Library: Jerry Harper 7 & 22, Nick Meers 10/11, 36,
Joe Cornish 75; Durham Wildlife Trust/M Richardson 11; Redcar & Cleveland
Borough Council 12, 51; Forest Life Picture Library/Forestry Commission 16, 30,
46; College Valley Estates Ltd 21; Mulgrave Estate 52; North York Moors National
Park Authority 58; Yorkshire Wildlife Trust 61; Archie Miles 66, 71, 77; St Ives Estate
72; Stuart Handley 80, 81, 83; Mark Feather 87

Site maps produced by Belvoir Cartographics and Design
Designed by Liz Bourne
Site entries written by Sheila Ashton, researched by Tim Hill, Diana Moss &
Lorraine Weeks
Edited by Graham Blight

Printed and bound by Printing Express Ltd., Hong Kong
All the paper used in this book is 100% recycled

HOW TO USE THIS BOOK

Covering a region that encompasses Yorkshire and the Northeast of England (excluding South Yorkshire, which is included in *Exploring Woodland Peak District and Central England*), this book is divided into four areas represented by key maps on pp18–19, 40–41, 62–63 and 78–79. The tree symbols on these maps denote the location of each wood. In the pages following the key maps, the sites nearest one another are described together (wherever practical) to make planning a day out as rewarding as possible.

For each site entry the name of the nearest town/village is given, followed by road directions and the grid reference of the site entrance. The area of the site (in hectares (HA) followed by acres) is given next together with the official status of the site where appropriate. The owner, body or organisation responsible for maintaining the site is given next. Symbols are used to denote information about the site and its facilities. These are explained on p17.

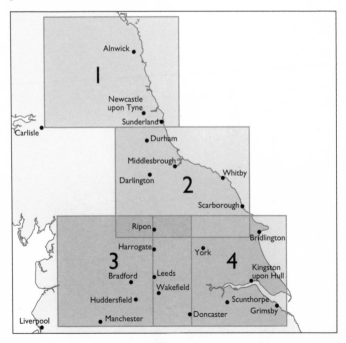

INTRODUCTION

Woodland Trust celebrity supporter, Alistair McGowan, says: 'Can you imagine what our countryside would look like without trees? Sound like a colourless and dreary place? Woods offer us peace and tranquillity, inspire our imagination and creativity, and refresh our souls. A land without trees would be a barren, cold and impoverished place. When I want to get back in touch with nature and escape from the hustle and bustle of my daily life, I love to visit and explore these natural treasures. These places are rich in wildlife and support a wide variety of animal and plant life. This excellent series of Woodland Trust guidebooks charts some of the most spectacular woods across the UK. You will be amazed and inspired to discover the wide variety of cultural and ecological history that exists in these special places. Each guide provides you with the all the information you will ever need.'

YORKSHIRE & THE NORTHEAST

'Don't go too close. Be careful. Hold my hand tightly.' My mother's anxiety recalled today as strongly as the clammy protective hand that kept me firmly away from trouble. My Yorkshire childhood brings back many fond memories, but none sweeter than those with a hint of danger. Balmy summer day trips in The Dales; chugging happily through the countryside in my grandma's peacock blue Morris 1000. One of our favourite days out was Bolton Abbey, skimming stones across the river, on to The Strid for a picnic lunch, and then tea and buns at Barden Tower.

The Strid certainly stuck in the mind more for its hazardous reputation rather than its glorious woodland setting. Here the tumbling waters of the River Wharfe are suddenly constricted by a narrow gritstone passage, not only very deep, but also undercut with many ledges beneath the surface. The estate brochure warns of the dangers of trying to jump the river here – '..remember that anything that goes into The Strid rarely surfaces for several days.' The forces of nature are formidable, but that said The Strid and its attendant woodlands with their excellent network of paths have been a lure for visitors for almost 200 years. In many respects this

Fine views extend beyond Bagger's wooded slopes, p76

Fern-lined waterfall in the garden at Cragside, p22

wood is typical of many other ancient woodlands in Yorkshire which have survived in the deeper, narrower valleys, where they have been safe from the marauding grazings of sheep and too inaccessible for agricultural development.

Around some of the larger cities such as Sheffield, Leeds and Bradford a handful of quite sizeable woods have endured mainly because they had some economic association with the city industries. An abundance of coppice woods, known in this region as 'spring woods', were constantly required to provide charcoal, tan bark, fuel wood and timber. Hetchell Wood, near Leeds, typifies many of these woodlands of the acidic gritstones with predominantly sessile oak and birch growing from a carpet of heaths, bilberry and bracken. Since most of these woods are no longer rigorously managed occasional plantings such as beech or blow-ins such as sycamore have added to the mix. Sycamore is a great coloniser, a pretty good habitat for many insects (plus the birds these attract), and a provider of excellent timber.

Understanding exactly how these woodlands have evolved all adds to the fascination, and this is merely one aspect of a wonderful woodland project currently under way near Bradford. The Royds Community Association, at Wyke, have put together one of the very best booklets dedicated to a single woodland that I've had the pleasure to read. Judy Woods is more than a single wood; in reality a group of several adjoining woods which line the Royds Hall Beck. The booklet takes you on a ramble through the history and evolution of the woods, laced with anecdotal tales of some of the

Trees in Nunsbrough Wood cling to the gorge sides, p34

colourful characters who frequented them. Judy Woods derives from Judy North who, in the 19th century, lived in the woods and sold 'sticks of spice, parkin pigs and ginger beer' to the many visitors. There are also tales of buried treasure and 'ghostly goings on' in the wood, much concerning its industrial past, as well as interpretation of the existing woodland structure and wildlife, and even a management strategy for the future. What more could you ask for? Projects like this are so crucial in urban areas where a true empathy with woodland and an appreciation of its huge importance as wildlife habitat can be nurtured within the community.

On the other side of the Leeds/Bradford conurbation a somewhat different urban woodland experience awaits. A few minutes from the dual carriageway of the A63, as it roars eastwards out of Leeds, lies the Temple Newsam Estate. Here, much of the woodland is in small, well-managed stands or clumps of fine specimen trees, which hark back to its 18th century landscaped heyday. The house is frequently used for fairs or functions. There are formal gardens, lakeside walks and loads of open space to play games, picnic or just snooze in the sun. A working farm, farm museum and rare breeds centre are also a great attraction for children. Yet again these old estates prove their supreme value as both marvellous amenities and green oases amidst the cut and thrust of city life.

Farther north and the Dales country is regained once more. In the upper reaches, where limestone prevails, some startling little woods adorn the deep cut gorges and gills, and few more spectacular than Thornton and Twisleton Glens above Ingleton. Torrents of water rushing off the fells have carved through the different types of rock forming giant steps over which dramatic falls cascade – Thornton Force perhaps the most impressive of all. Oak is the dominant tree here, with alder and willow along the waterside. The urban Victorians loved to explore wild and rugged countryside, and in the latter part of the nineteenth century a fast expanding rail system was eager to transport them to their rural idyll. In 1885 the most astute folks of Ingleton set up an 'improvement company' to build paths, construct bridges and provide seats along a Waterfall Walk. Visitors came in their thousands, and have kept coming to marvel ever since.

The landscape of this western reach of Yorkshire contrasts sharply with the softer undulating folds of the Yorkshire Wolds and the North York Moors in the east. In this more open country-side some of the largest tracts of woodland in Yorkshire are encountered, albeit much of it heavily coniferised. An unforgettable approach to the North York Moors from the west, takes the steep snaking road up Sutton Bank on to the Hambleton Hills (watch out for low flying gliders). At the top a National Park Visitor Centre makes a grand starting point for numerous bridleways and paths, notably the long distance Cleveland Way. The 'nature trail' path drops down into Garbutt Wood, which nestles between the thousand foot crags of Whitestone Cliff and an ancient lake with the spooky name of Gormire, believed to be a relic of the last ice age. Bluebells make a great show in springtime, but the stars here are the splendid old gnarled oaks and birches.

However, if it's truly ancient oaks you want to see then Duncombe Park, near the small market town of Helmsley, is the place to be. This fine ancestral home is surrounded by parkland largely created in the 18th century, which fortunately managed to employ much of the existing ancient wood-pasture into the schemes of that time. English Nature looks after the most sensitive parts of the site and permission must be sought to visit these areas which could not cope so well with mass visitor pressure. Here the vast crumbling oak pollards are many hundreds of years old and

Across the Derwent Valley toward Gibside's statue of liberty (l) and hall ruins (r), p36

the site is considered one of the most important in northern England for wood-feeding insects. The more formal parts of the parkland contain some equally spectacular specimen trees, such as the tallest Common lime in Britain at a majestic 44 metres (144 feet 4 inches).

Nearby Bridestones Moor, in the Dalby Forest, harbours some gargantuan rock formations, known locally as nabs, which Gerald Wilkinson once so aptly described as, 'Jurassic vol-au-vents of perhaps 200 tons apiece made by the giant Pastry Cook 150 million years ago.' These strange outcrops of sandstone are composed of a mixture of hard and soft layers which have been sculptured by wind, rain and frost erosion. Most of the surrounding woodland is part of a vast conifer plantation begun in 1919, but the Forestry Commission has now instigated new regimes to vary the tree age within stands, break up solid ranks of trees and encourage some of the smaller enclaves of broadleaves. Proof positive that these hills were once cloaked in a rich broadleaf mix has come from excavations of New Stone Age burial mounds here, beneath which the 5,000 year old remains of woodlands, once cleared for agriculture, have been detected.

For an altogether different view of the moors take a trip on the North York Moors Railway and steam sedately from Pickering to Grosmont along one of the finest scenic lines in the land.

Alternatively, dovetail a round trip on part of the railway with a good walk and a pint at one of the many fine hostelries around the moor.

The salt laden northeast coast of Yorkshire wouldn't appear to be very promising for woodlands, but tucked in some of the valleys a few gems await discovery. Mulgrave Woods, near Sandsend, lines two valleys on a private estate, where 200 years of management and artistry have created something special. Humphry Repton was brought in for a makeover (how did he fit

Low Barns Nature Reserve, a haven for wildlife, p45

Sunset at Errington Wood, p48

it all in, travelling the length and breadth of the country?). His legacy? Some wonderful vistas, decorative stone bridges and a rock tunnel, much of which is currently being restored to the original vision. The woodland is a healthy mixture of hard and softwoods, and seasonal delights include carpets of snowdrops, primroses and bluebells, as well as stunning autumn colours.

A little further up the coast, at Saltburn-by-the-Sea, there's another fine coastal valley woodland, so if it's too blustery for a walk on the front or too nippy for a dip in the briny try a walk through Rifts Wood in the Saltburn Valley – a fairly small wood with lots of year round interest and an excellent Woodland Centre, ideal for families and schools.

Rifts Wood is a very small part of a network of woodlands both new and old which have been designated as part of the Tees Forest, one of England's twelve Community Forests, which wraps its green way around the lower Tees valley. The other Community Forest within this region is the Great North Forest in County Durham and Tyneside. The aims of these forests are broadly similar; by planting anew and by better management of existing trees and woodland the main thrust is a greening of some of the more environmentally ravaged or neglected regions around urban conurbations and industrialised communities, and by revitalising these landscapes making them healthier and more pleasant places to live, work and play. The maturing forests will have both commercial and amenity value, and greatly improve habitat potential for wildlife.

On the northern tip of the Tees Forest lies Castle Eden Dene; a designated National Nature Reserve, at 222 hectares (549 acres) this is the largest area of ancient woodland in the northeast. Twelve miles of paths weave through this deep four mile gorge as it cuts through the Magnesian limestone towards the sea. Yews, which love the calcareous rocks grow here in profusion making a marvellous contrasting backdrop for the bright springtime foliage of the dominant ash. This is a superb site for wildlife – 300 different fungi are known to grow here and some 3,000 species of insect, although there are likely to be even more than this. Better still perhaps the thought that you may well see red squirrels scampering through the trees. Yet another of those public spirited Victorian clergymen, Rev. John Burdon, must be acknowledged for creating carriageways, footpaths and footbridges which originally opened up this magical place to visitors.

A stark contrast with the rugged gorge woodlands are those

Whitestone Cliff, a dramatic feature of Garbutt Wood, p61

Crystal waters tumble over rocks in Scaleber Wood, p64

legacies of the golden age of landscaping, when trees and woodland were but two strings to the grand designer's bow. Gibside, in the Derwent valley, has all the trees you could desire, both natives and exotics, plus a Palladian Chapel, Column of Liberty, Orangery, Walled Garden and Banqueting House,.... oh yes, and some romantic ruins; and all this is very handy if you live in the Newcastle metropolis.

Northumberland contains woods on contrasting scales. While the country's largest wooded forest is to be found at Kielder, three quarters of the county's other woods are less than ten hectares in size. However, amongst these there are some great little woods and, as expected, often found in steep secluded valleys.

West of Hexham find the Allen valley with its network of inter-linked woods; Allen Banks, Staward Gorge and Briarwood Banks. Exploring this valley will unearth the remains of a medieval pele tower and gatehouse, evidence of coal and lead mining and three lime kilns. There's a manmade network of 'Wilderness Walks' created between 1830 and 1860, with suspension bridges spanning the torrent below. A wide variety of native broadleaves are present as well as planted beech and conifers. There's an unusual floral treasure to be found in a meadow where wild pansies beam brightly from the sward amongst a stand of conifers, and you may care to know (although you'll be very lucky to see one) that this is the northern most habitat for the dormouse.

Closer to Hexham a heartwarming springtime picture awaits at Letah Wood, near Newbiggin, where a fine show of wild daffodils make the woodland floor glow. This is thought to be the last stronghold in Northumberland of these dainty little flowers of ancient woodland.

For flowers of an altogether more overpowering nature look no further than the banks of rhododendrons at Cragside, a National Trust property near Rothbury, where house and garden were the creations of the first Lord Armstrong, a great Victorian innovator and industrialist. A great day out for families here, with walks aplenty, formal gardens to admire, an adventure playground and, of course, an excellent cafe and shop. Cragside holds a special place in history as the first house in the world to have been lit by hydro-electricity, and the lakes at the top of the estate, as well as the waterwheel which they powered, can all still be seen. A superb collection of trees combines impressive native specimens with a host of conifers from around the world, either set within the rugged natural landscape or adorning some of the dramatic manmade vistas.

A complete contrast, far from the company of others, in one of the remotest parts of Northumberland, is a day spent exploring

Steps enable the visitor to explore Nidd Gorge, p84

A corner of Spurlswood, part of Hamsterley Forest, p46

the College valley, not far from Wooler. This great open space beneath the Cheviot Hills offers purple heather clad moors, little white farmsteads dotting the landscape, and woodlands either of conifers or, along the valley sides, fragments of ancient broadleaf. This is wild and woolly country where you must keep your wits about you – no bears or wolves here (yet), but the weather can sometimes take a turn for the worse quite rapidly, so set out well equipped and well informed.

The northeast of England may not be the most wooded area of Britain, and while many of the finest woods may seem remote or inaccessible, they most definitely reward those with the desire and energy to seek them out and once discovered they will prove a source of pleasure at any time of year.

Archie Miles

Quick Reference

Symbols used to denote information about each site and the facilities to be found there.

Type of wood

🔲 Mainly broadleaved woodland

🔺 Mainly coniferous woodland

🔲 Mixed woodland

Car Park

🅿 Parking on site

🅿 Parking nearby

🅿 Parking difficult to find

Status

AONB Area of Outstanding Natural Beauty

SSSI Site of Special Scientific Interest

NP National Park

Site Facilities

▊ Sign at entry

ℹ Information board

♿ One or more paths suitable for wheelchair users

🐕 Dogs allowed under supervision

▱ Waymarked trail

🚻 Toilet

⛱ Picnic area

£ Entrance/car park charge

🍴 Refreshments on site

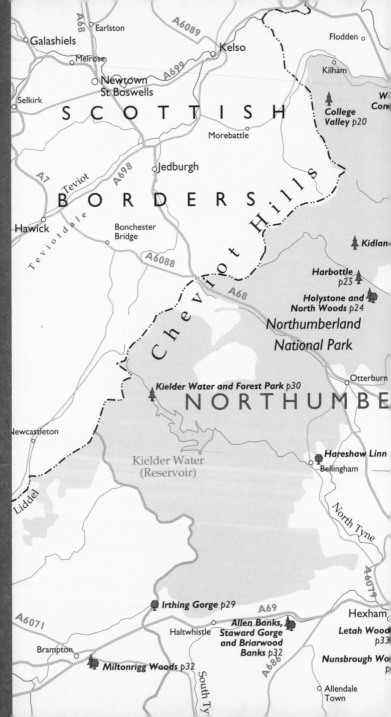

Galashiels
Earlston
A68
A6089
Flodden
Kelso
Melrose
Kilham
A699
Newtown
St Boswells
A699
W
Selkirk
Con
SCOTTISH
College
Valley p20
A7
Morebattle
Teviot
A698
Jedburgh
BORDERS
Kidlan
Hawick
Bonchester
Bridge
A6088
Harbottle
p25
Teviotdale
A68
Holystone and
North Woods p24
Northumberland
Cheviot Hills
National Park
Otterburn
Kielder Water and Forest Park p30
NORTHUMBE
Newcastleton
Hareshaw Linn
Kielder Water
(Reservoir)
Bellingham
Liddel
North Tyne
A6079
A6071
Irthing Gorge p29
Hexham
A69
Allen Banks,
Letah Wood
Staward Gorge
p33
Haltwhistle
and Briarwood
Banks p32
Brampton
Nunsbrough Wo
p
Miltonrigg Woods p32
A686
Allendale
Town
South Ty

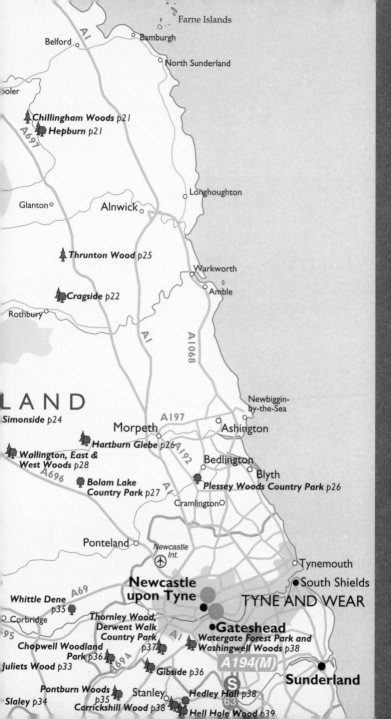

College Valley

Wooler

Follow A697 north from Wooler take
B6351 west towards Kirknewton. Hamlet
after Kirknewton is Westnewton. Take
minor road left at Westnewton towards
Hethpool. Follow road until it ends at
cattle grid. Parking in field at beginning of
College Valley. Use of the road beyond the
car park is by permit only. (NT895285)
4,800HA (11,864ACRES) SSSI NP
College Valley Estates Ltd

Stamina and determination pay
dividends for visitors to College
Valley in Northumberland
National Park, a site so large
and remote that reaching and
exploring it takes a little effort.
The best way to explore this
beautiful landscape is to arrive
early and spend all day
walking, cycling or riding
along its 28-mile web of footpaths and bridleways.

The woodland, surrounded
by the bold, dramatic
landscape of the Cheviot Hills,
rises from Hethpool Lakes
towards the summit of Cheviot.

This valley of contrasts has
many different habitats, colours
and textures set beneath rapidly
changing skies. Scattered conifer
plantations clad parts of the
hillside, with deciduous woodland, heather moorland, swathes
of bracken and farmland
painting a patchwork on the
landscape. College Burn, heavily
camouflaged by scrub, runs
through the centre of the valley.

It is worth noting that
because of rapid weather
changes, visitors are
recommended to leave route
details in their car.

Wooler Common

Wooler

Heading south on A697 (South Road)
turn right into The Perth. Turn left into
Ramsey Lane which continues into
Common Road. Woods and car park on
right. Brown tourist signs from A697
and town centre. (NT980277)
81HA (200ACRES)
Forestry Commission

Wooler Common Woodland
Park, in the heart of the Cheviot
Hills, has a wild beauty that
masks a turbulent history.

An open common, it is
enveloped by well managed
community woodland where
standard trees are planted as
tributes to local people.

Marauding Scots targeted the
area between the 14th and 16th
centuries but it is on the common
that most historical evidence
remains. The relics of a hill top
fort stand close to Pin Well,
where young ladies would
make a wish for love on May
Day. Overlooking it is the King's
Chair, a rocky outcrop where a

Chillingham

Scottish king is said to have observed a battle and from where visitors can enjoy more stunning – but serene – views of the surrounding countryside.

The site is criss-crossed by a network of well maintained paths and there are two trails, one wheelchair-friendly route, dotted with willow sculptures, that circles Humbleton Burn where wildfowl can be spotted on two ponds.

This popular local beauty spot is a site to savour, to listen and look as you explore a site that is bursting with wildlife.

If you tread carefully among the mixed conifer and broadleaf woodland look for signs of roe and fallow deer, red squirrels, foxes, badgers and hares that all thrive here. It is also possible to spot birds such as buzzard, green and greater spotted woodpeckers, goshawks, nuthatch and even crossbill.

The woodland sits within the stunning landscape of the Cheviots in north Northumberland, not too far from the Scottish Border and is perfect for walkers who can enjoy a series of way-marked routes through the site.

While you won't be able to spy the fabulous famed beasts of nearby Chillingham Wild Cattle Park from the woodland, guided walks are available.

Chillingham Woods

Chillingham

Follow A697 south taking B6348 left at Wooler. At the village of Chatton take right towards Chillingham. Along this road turn off left to Chillingham, woods are on the right. (NU063260)
250HA (618ACRES)
College Valley Estates Ltd

Hepburn

Alnwick

Follow A697 south, turning left onto B6348 at Wooler. At the village of Chatton take right towards Chillingham. Go past Chillingham and take left turn minor road to Hepburn. Woods are 1.6km (1 mile) on right. (NU073248)
102HA (252ACRES)
Forestry Commission

Cragside

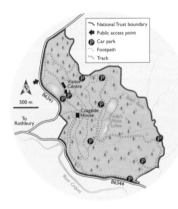

Rothbury

21km (13 miles) southwest of Alnwick (B6341) and 24km (15 miles) northwest of Morpeth on Wooler road (A697), turn left on to B6341 at Moorhouse Crossroads, entrance 1.6km (1 mile) north of Rothbury. (NU073022) 400HA (989ACRES)
The National Trust

There is a huge, wild feel to Cragside, a large estate where tall trees stand among huge rock outcrops and with lots of different woodland walks to explore.

This is truly a place of wonder. It was created by the great Victorian innovator and industrialist Lord Armstrong, who transformed a bare hillside into a riot of rhododendron – that blazes in full bloom during late May and June – and exotic trees.

A total of seven million trees and shrubs were planted to create the 1,000-acre forest garden that is still providing magic more than a century on.

The efforts of man and Nature combine at Cragside, with magnificent views of the estate and surrounding countryside and an impressive range of veteran trees to inspire the mind – including a Douglas fir, towering pines and formal plantings. England's tallest tree can be found in the pinetum on the estate, which can be explored via miles of footpaths and drives.

Two large lakes at the top of the estate once powered a waterwheel to provide electricity for the Victorian house – the first in the world lit by hydro-electricity. Described as 'the Palace of a Modern Magician', the 1880s' property was well ahead of its time, with hot and cold running water, fire alarms, telephones, a Turkish bath suite and even a passenger lift.

The house is surrounded by one of Europe's largest rock gardens while across the valley is a terraced garden where exotic fruits were nurtured year-round in glasshouses – as they are today in the Orchard House.

The estate features a six-mile drive so it is possible to get a good feel for the estate without leaving the car. Those exploring on foot are advised to wear stout footwear to enable you to tackle a series of steps and sharp gradients.

Simonside

Harwood

From Rothbury take B6342 south. Turn
right following sign to Simonside.
Follow minor road for 5km (3 miles),
forest on left. (NZ037996)
2,954HA (7,301ACRES)
Forestry Commission

There is a wild and rugged
beauty to Simonside, a mature
forest rising up the dark slopes
of the Simonside Hills which
dominate the middle reaches of
Coquetdale.

Simonside is the haunt of
serious walkers but there is a
fine reward for those who
tackle the challenging 6.5 km
(4 miles) climb to Simonside
Ridge where moorland birds
such as red grouse and ring
ouzel nestle. Here you can
enjoy stunning and dramatic
views of the Cheviots and,
on a clear day, the entire
Northumbrian coastline.

Those who don't make it to
the summit can enjoy a walk
through the forest by choosing
one of the less-challenging
waymarked routes including a
1.6 km (1 mile) walk from the
car park through post World
War II larch plantations.

Ravensheugh is a strenuous
walk of 7km (4.5 miles) taking
a steady climb through pine
plantations with silver birch
and rowan, past a 4,000-year
old Bronze Age burial cairn,
emerging onto open moorland.

Holystone and North Woods

Holystone Village

On the A696 south turn left near
Otterburn onto B6341. Take next minor
road left to Harbottle and next left to
Holystone, car park on left.
(NT950024)
209HA (517ACRES) SSSI NP
Forestry Commission

Tucked away in a quiet corner
of Coquetdale you will
discover the beauty, peace and
tranquillity of Holystone Wood.

The village of Holystone
evolved around a 12th-century
nunnery, now gone, but its
atmosphere of remoteness can
still be enjoyed with beautiful
walks and a rich natural and
historical heritage.

A commercial plantation,
Holystone is also a popular
recreation spot with contrasting
landscapes and views. One
moment you are in dense
woodland or plantation, with
lichens and mosses dripping
off the trees and the next
emerging into open moorland
and farmland.

Three waymarked routes
vary from forest rides to
challengingly muddy paths.

The longest of the walks, at 8km (5 miles), leads deep into the forest plantations to Holystone Common and Dove Crags. A shorter Farm Walk skirts the ancient woodland of North Wood while the shortest of the walks follows the route of a former Roman road out onto farmland and Lady's Well.

While in the area you may like to extend your walk to include Harbottle Wood, which adjoins Holystone.

Miltonrigg Woods, p32

Harbottle (West Wood)

Harbottle
On the A696 south turn left near Otterburn into B6341. Take next minor road left to Harbottle. Go through Harbottle, woods are on left. (NT927048)
599HA (1,480ACRES) SSSI NP
Forestry Commission

Thrunton Wood

Thrunton and Rothbury
Follow brown tourist signs off the A697, just north of the intersection with the B6341 Rothbury to Alnwick road. (NU085097)
1,135HA (2,805ACRES)
Forestry Commission

Kidland

Rothbury
Take A68 south. B6341 towards Rotherby then minor road to Alwinton. Use National Park car park in Alwinton village and walk to wood. (NT917105)
1,113HA (2,751ACRES) NP
Forestry Commission

Hartburn Glebe

Hartburn Glebe

Hartburn

Take B6343 turning off A1 (near
Morpeth) and follow toward Cambo.
The wood is on the right and there is a
small lay-by at the first entrance.
(NZ088864)

3HA (8 ACRES)

The Woodland Trust

It is easy to see why writers have
waxed lyrical about romantic
Hartburn Glebe since the 18th
century.

Set in an area 'of great
landscape value', this beautiful
wood sustains a rich variety of
wildlife including red squirrels,
badgers and otters and an
abundance of wild garlic, woodrush and yellow pimpernel.

History, as well as Nature,
beckons experts and casual
visitors alike to Hartburn
Glebe. A deep natural hole in
the stream bed on the wood's
northeastern side was said to
conceal silver and valuables
snatched in Viking raids and
the famed Roman road the
Devil's Causeway crossed Hart
Burn, where goosanders, heron
and the occasional kingfisher
are spotted today.

Another magical attraction is
a wonderful Grade II listed
grotto, linked to the river by a
tunnel which was adapted for
the use of bathers. There is also
an elaborate sandstone bridge
and a series of walkways
fashioned by 18th-century
Hartburn vicar, the Rev.
Doctor Sharpe.

Plessey Woods Country Park

Bedlington

Take the A1068 south of Bedlington and
wood is on right. Or, heading north from
Newcastle on A1, take A19 junction
then A1068 toward Ashington. Approaching

Hartburn Bridge, Plessey is signed to left just after bridge. (NZ240800)
40HA (100ACRES)
Northumberland County Council

People have been flocking to Plessey Woods for generations to enjoy the woods and river. Plessey offers the chance to escape life's stresses by getting close to Nature.

Known locally as Bluebell Woods, this is the ideal place for a family day out. The woodland sustains an array of birds including the greater spotted woodpecker, nuthatch and tree creeper while red squirrel, fox and roe deer also make their presence known.

The banks of the River Blyth provide a wonderful habitat for kingfishers, dippers and otters – keep alert and you might spot one.

There is a world of recreation opportunities to choose from, including fishing, riding, orienteering, cycling, canoeing and of course, walking with many self-guided trails laid out. A guide has been produced to help people with mobility difficulties get the most out of their visit. Refreshments are available from the cafe on site, open each weekend and school holidays.

Bolam Lake Country Park

Belsay
Signposted off A696 near Belsay.
(NZ083820)
40HA (99ACRES)
Northumberland County Council

An assortment of self-guided trails, available from the visitor centre, helps people get the most out of a day at this well-used park.

The impressive man-made 25 acre lake was created in 1818 and today attracts an impressive range of birdlife including resident mute swans. If you arrive in winter with bird food, hungry blue tits can be fed by hand in the clearings beside the car parks.

Bolam Lake Country Park caters for a range of interests. In summer, families take picnics on the meadows while others enjoy the cool shade by following a variety of woodland walks. The lake meanwhile is busy with fishermen and canoeists.

Two other woods of interest and an historic property are close by. Wallington (see next page) is considered one of the most stunning woodland sites in the northeast to visit. Also not far away are Hartburn Glebe and Belsay Castle and Hall with its magnificent 30-acre gardens.

Wallington, East & West Woods

Morpeth

Heading southeast on A696 turn right onto B6342 to Cambo. Follow this road for 4km (2.5 miles), wood is on left. (NZ030843)

45HA (111ACRES)

The National Trust

Venture into the heart of beautiful rural Northumberland to encounter one of the most accessible and stunning woodland sites the northeast has to offer.

Wallington, East and West Woods form part of the Wallington estate, home of the Trevelyan family and full of interest including parkland, walled gardens, imaginative woodland sculptures and water features.

Ever changing scenery, the woods go from open parkland dotted with native and exotic species to open beech woodland followed by dense conifer plantation and regenerating ash.

East and West Woods are mixed deciduous woodlands with ponds and waterways, a good network of well kept footpaths and seating where visitors can enjoy peaceful rests. A wildlife hide in West Wood gives the chance to spot deer, birds and red squirrels by Middle Pond.

For a really adventurous walk, follow the trails through West Wood, along the River Wansbeck and up into the walled garden, returning to the hall via East Wood.

Hareshaw Linn

Bellingham

From A69 Newcastle to Carlisle road, take A6079 from west of Hexham and follow B6320 to Bellingham. Turn right half way through Bellingham after town hall and shops (just before tourist information on left). Go down hill and over bridge. Car park on left opposite police station. (NY842846)

20HA (49ACRES) SSSI

Northumberland

National Park Authority

Steeped in natural beauty and a rich industrial heritage, Hareshaw Linn is a broadleaf valley woodland with a magnificent waterfall as its focal point.

The woodland – a mixture of oak and ash with a hazel understorey and the occasional Scots pine and Douglas fir, a legacy of the Victorians, has been loved by generations of local people. An impressive 300 different mosses, lichens and liverworts thrive in the wood and can be seen cloaking the trees.

Six bridges, one of them hand-crafted, cross the Linn and add to the quality of this stunning setting. Many remnants of the former ironworks that once dominated the valley can be found and the quarry workings have left a lime-rich soil in which plants such as fairy flax are thriving.

Irthing Gorge

Gilsland

Either park in the village of Gilsland and follow the public footpath which passes Wardrew House or turn off B6318 in Gilsland toward Gilsland Spa. If you can find a space to park near the hotel you can walk into the wood from here. (NY634685)

34HA (84 ACRES) SSSI NP

The Woodland Trust

History, romance, spectacular scenery, watersports and an abundance of wildlife – Irthing Gorge has it all.

This ancient woodland, a site of special scientific interest in the Northumberland National Park, forms part of a mosaic of wildlife habitats. It lines the steep sides of a deep gorge chiselled by the fast-flowing River Irthing. At its head is a waterfall known as Crammel Linn. Now the Woodland Trust is planting native trees on adjoining grassland to buffer and extend the ancient woodland.

Red squirrels and badgers inhabit the gorge, alongside a varied bird population and a rich mix of woodland plants. Yew grows on the cliff edges while ash dominates the lower slopes and birch is to be found on higher ground.

The gorge lies 6.5km (4 miles) north of Gilsland, one of 19th-century Britain's most fashionable spa resorts. Still popular, its scenery is as romantic as ever.

Irthing Gorge

Kielder Water and Forest Park

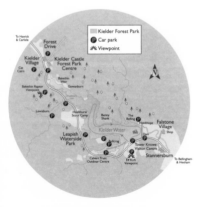

Kielder

From A69 at Hexham take A6079 north then left onto B6318 for short distance. Follow B6320 to Bellingham, then minor road signed to Kielder. (NY632935)

60,000HA (148,295ACRES) SSSI NP

Forestry Commission

One of Britain's biggest nature resorts, vast Kielder Forest and Kielder Water is full of wild northern romance and magic.

Although quite remote this enormous site is hugely popular, attracting more than a quarter of a million visitors a year, thereby making it one of Northumberland's top five tourist attractions. But the 250 square mile expanse is capable of absorbing large numbers of people. You could spend a week here without feeling crowded.

For a sense of freedom and vast expanses of space, enjoy the vistas across Kielder Water, Europe's largest man-made lake – it will fill you with awe. But the reservoir is not the only star – it shares the glory with the woodland.

If you have ever hankered to see remote working forests on a large scale, this is the place to be. Vast expanses of plantations – 150 million standing trees – can be seen at all levels of maturity within a mammoth forest producing 1,300 tonnes of timber a day.

Brimming with red squirrels, deer and birds, this giant nature reserve includes no fewer than eight designated sites of special scientific interest. The woodland is dominated by Sitka spruce and pine but there is a broadleaf presence here and with a planting programme in hand, the percentage of hardwoods on the site is expected to increase over the next decade and a half.

Size is not everything and there are ample opportunities to enjoy walks in small areas of woodland and plantations, relish the sight of ferns dripping with dew, soak in the sights of wonderful outdoor sculptures including the 'Cat Cairn' Kielder Skyspace structure. Visit in daylight to enjoy the natural light being funnelled into this intriguing chamber through a perfect circle above. Two hours before dawn and after dusk, visitors are treated to an internal display of lights, activated on entrance. You are also advised to take a torch at these times.

Lots of routes means lots of choice. The forest drive goes east to west through the heart of the forest and there are countless tracks for foot, horseback or cycling access. If you prefer to have your day organised, there is a host of events to choose from.

Allen Banks, Staward Gorge and Briarwood Banks

Haydon Bridge

6.5km (4 miles) west of Haydon Bridge on the A69, turn south onto minor road signed Allen Banks. Having crossed river, take left fork and follow road to National Trust Allen Banks car park. To reach Briarwood Banks either walk along river from Allen Banks car park or follow signs to Plankey Mill and park at farm (NY791620). Cross river bridge to reserve. Staward Gorge can be accessed from either car park. (NY797640/NY791620) 200HA (494ACRES) SSSI

The National Trust/
Northumberland Wildlife Trust

Popular with walkers, these woods flank the deep-sided slopes along the River Allen and its tributary valleys.

Dormice, red squirrel, otter, roe deer, badger, mink and stoat are among the animals at home here, together with more than 60 species of bird.

A network of occasionally steep and muddy paths leads through the woodland and beside the river. Try the 4km (2.5 mile) route from Allen Banks car park through Victorian ornamental woodland to Plankey Mill – this encompasses the entire site. More adventurous visitors can continue to Staward Gorge, a more rugged area to the south, to look for the ruins of a medieval pele tower and gate-house.

Woodlands here are largely ancient with oak and wych elm growing above a rich ground flora including moschatel, while 18th-century beech and conifers prevail elsewhere. One of the joys of this site is encountering the meadow where wild pansies grow adjacent to a stand of conifers at Allen Banks.

Miltonrigg Woods

Brampton

A69 from Brampton, turn right on minor road heading south, car park 30m on right. (NY559612) 63HA (157ACRES)

The Woodland Trust

A full entry for this site appears in the *Exploring Woodland Guide to the Lake District and Northwest England*.

Letah Wood

Letah Wood

Hexham

Taking B6306 from Hexham, turn right
signed Newbiggin. In Newbiggin turn
right into Hill Road, the main entrance
to the wood and car park is on the left.
(NY939604)
14 HA (35 ACRES)
The Woodland Trust

See Letah Wood in early spring
and you'll be greeted by the
rare and wonderful sight of wild
daffodils – a clue to its ancient
origins. And whenever you visit
you'll hear the bubbling sounds
of Letah Burn as it tumbles by.

Thought to be Northumber-
land's last wild daffodil wood,
Letah has witnessed their numbers
increasing over recent decades.

Once part of the Newbiggin
Estate, which dates back to the
14th century, woods have
existed here for centuries. The
original cover of oak, ash and
elm was supplemented with
non-native trees such as beech
and conifers and, since the 19th
century, the wood has been a
mixture of broadleaves and
conifers. Seek out, in particular,
the massive specimens of beech
and Douglas fir.

Red squirrels share the wood
with roe deer, fox and stoat and
a bird population that includes
jay, wagtail, hawfinch, redwing
and blackcap.

Juliets Wood

Hexham

From A695 east of Hexham, take B6307
to Slaley/Blanchland. Turn left at
T-junction with B6306 and left again
into Slaley village and park on left near
bungalows. Follow footpath north to
Marley Cote Walls and the wood is
reached after approx 1km. (NY977587)
8HA (20ACRES)
Northumberland Wildlife Trust

Nunsbrough Wood

Ordley

Follow B6306 south of Hexham, turning right for Newbiggin and then follow signs for Ordley. There are three public entrances to the wood: main entrance is from Ordley village, another is from the south on the public footpath that leads through the wood and a further one from the north across Linnelswood Bridge. (NY950595)

16 HA (40 ACRES)

The Woodland Trust

The twists and turns of Devil's Water, south of Hexham, adds drama to Nunsbrough Wood which lines the steep slopes of the gorge.

Although secluded, the woodland is served by a way-marked public footpath running north to south. A permissive path leads down to the large riverside

Whittle Dene

meadow where summer grazing encourages many flowers including the scented meadow sweet, lady's smock and lady's mantle.

The flow in this section of the Devil's Water is highly active. The resulting bank-side erosion creates a natural yet rare habitat.

The woodland itself is dominated by mature oak and ash planted in the 1920s, with two additional areas planted more recently north and south of the meadows.

Small clusters of alder line the more fertile, wet ground at the base of the slopes alongside sycamore, lime, horse chestnut and elm. A variety of ferns and flora provide attractive ground cover including dog's mercury, yarrow, pignut, wood sorrel and germander speedwell.

Slaley

Colpitts Grange

In centre of Hexham take B6306 signed Slaley. Carry on past Slaley village. Car park on right just after entering forest. (NY978552)

511HA (1,263ACRES)

Forestry Commission

Pontburn Woods

Hamsterley Mill
Take A692 from A1 and follow south toward Consett. At Burnopfield take B6310 towards Hamsterley Mill. Small car park on right just before bridge over the Pont Burn at Hamsterley Mill. Access to woods across road from car park. (NZ145551)
91HA (225 ACRES)
The Woodland Trust

An important feature on the Derwent Valley landscape, Pontburn Woods are popular with local people, who enjoy good access via a comprehensive path network.

Dissected by the Derwent Walk, the site is actually a mosaic of conifer high forest and broadleaves, including ancient woodland and represents one of the valley's largest remaining areas of deciduous woodland.

Nuthatches number among a healthy population of breeding birds which thrive, along with many rare insects, including the Brown Lacewing.

Most of the woodland grows on the slopes straddling Pont Burn, one of a number of watercourses that flow through the woods. Alder grows in the wetter areas, whilst drier slopes consist largely of oak and birch. Come spring, wood-sorrel, bluebell and wood anemone add their colour.

Whittle Dene

Ovingham
Park in village and follow public footpath beside mill buildings and head northwest. Path enters wood at its southern boundary. (NZ072656)
20HA (49 ACRES)
The Woodland Trust

Set in a countryside haven, Whittle Dene is one of the first stretches of wooded land you come across when travelling west of Newcastle.

Wildlife thrives in this secluded piece of ancient woodland. The range of plant and insect life here benefits from coppicing which allows more light to reach the woodland floor and thereby encourages flowers.

The site is home to breeding sparrowhawks, red squirrels, deer and, it is believed, even otters. Bats and birdlife – including willow warbler, kestrel and owl – help bring the woods to life at night.

Whittle Dene has an industrial past. At the southern end of the wood are the remains of a mill pond, a well, weir structures and derelict buildings – all that's left of a water-driven flourmill. The mill pond has since been colonised with willow and alder.

Chopwell Woodland Park

High Spen
From A1 take A694 south. After
Rowlands Gill take B6315 right towards
High Spen. Wood is a couple of miles
on the left. (NZ139589)
375HA (927ACRES)
Forestry Commission

Walkers, cyclists and riders from
nearby Tyne and Wear enjoy the
many facilities provided at
Chopwell Woodland Park.

A conifer plantation with
mixed deciduous woodland in
places, it offers solitude and
tranquillity as well as exercise.

Yet human activity doesn't
prevent the park from bristling
with wildlife, supporting more
than 250 plant species, 95 different types of bird and a variety of mammals including red
squirrel and roe deer.

Gibside

The forest has a long history
of fueling the northeast's ship
building, coal mining and
bridge building industries and
remains a working wood with
pine, larch and fir still felled
for their timber. The remains
of a mineral railway features
on one of the woodland walks.

A range of waymarked trails
offer good access through this well-
managed forest, where creative
sculptures add extra interest. A
highlight of the programme is the
not-to-be-missed Chopwell Forest
Festival – a popular event each July
which attracts thousands of visitors.

Gibside

Rowlands Gill
Entrance on B6314 between
Burnopfield and Rowlands Gill. From
A1 take exit north of Metro Centre and
follow brown tourism signs. (NZ172583)
163HA (403ACRES) SSSI
The National Trust

One of the northeast's finest examples of 18th-century landscapes, Gibside in the Derwent Valley is a beautiful park and pleasure ground – and just a stone's throw from Gateshead and Newcastle.

This is a park for people. It provides a spectacular backcloth for a year-round programme of events and the visitors who flock to take part are well served with information, shopping and refreshment facilities and a landscape with a real 'genteel' feeling.

There is a mixture of deciduous woodland, dense conifer plantations and columns of exotic parkland trees. The Gibside Tree Trail details the changing landscapes through the ages. Four waymarked walks range from short walks hugging the car park to more challenging hikes up towards the Column of Liberty, one of a host of features standing out among the trees.

Other highlights include the Palladian Chapel and Long Walk, the walled garden, banqueting house and the ruins of Gibside Hall.

Thornley Wood, Derwent Walk Country Park

Rowlands Gill

From A1 take A694 south towards Rowlands Gill. Pass The Golden Lion pub on left and follow road until visitor centre sign for Thornley Woodland Centre on left. (NZ178603)

60HA (150ACRES) SSSI

Gateshead Council

A short journey from the urban buzz of Gateshead or Newcastle is one of the northeast's most outstanding ancient woodlands.

With a strong history as a working wood, the site is populated by oak, ash and hazel coppice and at its colourful best in spring, with a riot of bluebells, lesser celandine and ramsons.

A perfect complement to a stroll through the woods is neighbouring Derwenthaugh Park, a former cokeworks planted recently with thousands of trees. Fully accessible to walkers and cyclists alike, it provides the perfect entrance to the woodlands via the Derwent Walk, a former mineral line.

The Country Park boasts two observation hides, perfect for the dawn chorus, and a full events programme, available from the information centre.

Watergate Forest Park and Washingwell Woods

Gateshead

Follow signs off A1 to Lobley Hill and A692. Car park (offering wheelchair access) at top of Lobley Hill on Whickham Highway (B6317) beside Gateshead Central Nursery. Small car park beside Emmanuel College on A692. (NZ222598)

Gateshead Metropolitan Borough Council

Carrickshill Wood

Stanley

Take A6076 south from Gateshead towards Stanley. Opposite right turn to Causey Arch, turn left by pub/hotel into Beamishburn Road. Take first minor road on left at small white cottage. Car park signed Beamish Burn picnic site, 200m on right. (NZ204546) 10HA (25ACRES)

Durham County Council

Just a few miles from the centre of bustling Gateshead, Carrickshill Wood is a delightful combination of woodland set in a lovely landscape.

Great for families, it has a picnic area, space to play and a beautiful stream. But the main attraction is the woodland, a mix of 30 to 40-year-old conifer plantations and distinctive oaks, ashes and willows that date back 200 or 300 years. At the heart of the Great North Forest, Carrickshill is wonderful in spring with its white carpet of ramsons and for autumn colour.

A descriptive walk leads through the woods as part of the Tyne and Wear Trail with interpretation boards describing different tree species along the way. While not all the site is accessible there is still ample opportunity to enjoy the beauty of the setting.

With Beamish Museum just 1km away, why not combine a visit to Carrickshill with half a day at Beamish for a fun day out.

Hedley Hall

Sunniside

From Stanley follow A6076 north. After passing Causey station on left take next turning right. Car park on right. (NZ218559) 55HA (136 ACRES) SSSI

The Woodland Trust

Visitors flock to Hedley Hall Woods, a flagship site in the Great North Forest and a favourite for informal recreation and community events.

The woods occupy a tranquil setting close to Beamish Museum and are made up of Ridley Gill, a SSSI ancient

Hell Hole Wood

Beamish
Follow signs for Beamish Open Air Museum. As you leave the A693 at the roundabout, heading to the museum entrance, parking is on the left. From the corner of the car park a track leads eastwards towards the wood. (NZ209540)
19HA (48 ACRES)
The Woodland Trust

Hedley Hall

woodland, and a woodland creation scheme where broadleaved trees and shrubs have been planted on former arable and pasture land.

Running along the western edge, you can see the varied canopy of Ridley Gill rising out of the valley. Here are three distinct high forest woodland types – oak and the regionally uncommon wet alder and ash-elm woodland. Tussock sedge grows in abundance in the wet alder woodland.

Set on gently undulating land, Hedley Hall includes a large hay and wild flower meadow, a peat bog and a large glade where visitors can relax. Look for sculptured wooden seats and artwork along the Sculpture Trail which runs through the site.

Local people love to relax and play in Hell Hole Wood, a popular site within the Great North Forest.

However it is the red squirrel that may help to shape the future of this ancient woodland site close to Beamish in County Durham. A survey indicates that large numbers think this is not such a Hell Hole.

This has caused the Woodland Trust to re-think plans to fell the Japanese larch, Corsican pine, Scots pine and Douglas fir that dominate the site today, as part of a programme to restore its native broadleaves.

A Sustrans cycleway runs along the southern boundary of this wood. Access to the wood is by a good network of permissive footpaths and a public footpath through the northwest section. The main path leads into adjoining Carrickshill Wood.

Three small burns flow through the wood, chief of them being Letch Burn.

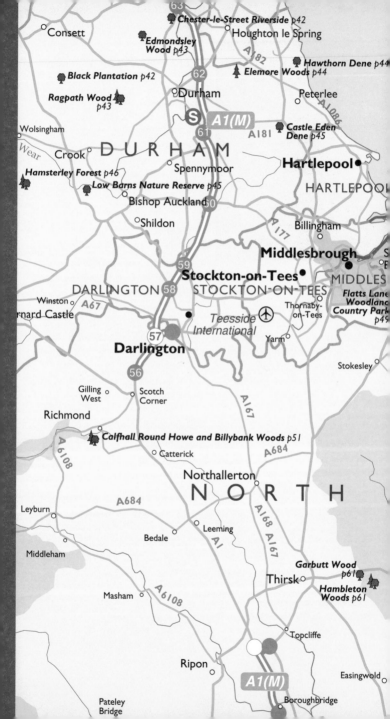

Consett

Chester-le-Street Riverside p42
Houghton le Spring

Edmondsley Wood p43

Hawthorn Dene p44
Elemore Woods p44

Black Plantation p42

Durham

Peterlee

Ragpath Wood p43

Wolsingham

S A1(M)

Castle Eden Dene p45

Wear Crook D U R H A M

A181

Hamsterley Forest p46

Spennymoor

Hartlepool

HARTLEPOOL

Low Barns Nature Reserve p45

Bishop Auckland

Shildon

Billingham

Middlesbrough

Stockton-on-Tees

MIDDLES

DARLINGTON

STOCKTON-ON-TEES

Winston A67

Flatts Lane Woodland Country Park p49

rnard Castle

Thornaby-on-Tees

Teesside International

Yarm

Darlington

Stokesley

Gilling West

Scotch Corner

Richmond

A6108

Calfhall Round Howe and Billybank Woods p51

Catterick

A684

Northallerton

N O R T H

Leyburn

A684

A168 A167

A1

Bedale

Leeming

Middleham

Garbutt Wood p61

Masham

A6108

Thirsk

Hambleton Woods p61

Topcliffe

Ripon

A1(M)

Easingwold

Pateley Bridge

Boroughbridge

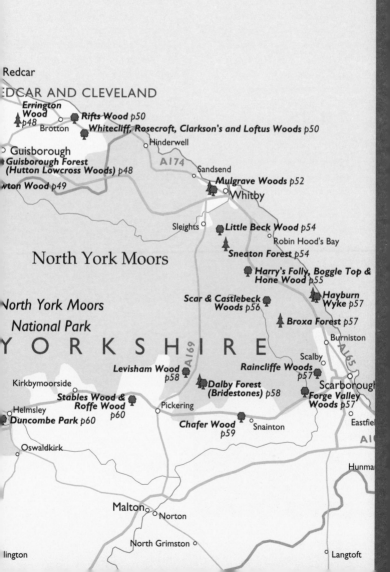

Redcar

REDCAR AND CLEVELAND

Errington Wood p48

Rifts Wood p50

Brotton

Whitecliff, Rosecroft, Clarkson's and Loftus Woods p50

Hinderwell

A174

Sandsend

Guisborough

Guisborough Forest (Hutton Lowcross Woods) p48

...ton Wood p49

Mulgrave Woods p52

Whitby

Sleights

Little Beck Wood p54

Robin Hood's Bay

North York Moors

Sneaton Forest p54

Harry's Folly, Boggle Top & Hone Wood p55

Scar & Castlebeck Woods p56

Hayburn Wyke p57

North York Moors National Park

Broxa Forest p57

Burniston

Y O R K S H I R E

A169

Scalby

A165

Levisham Wood p58

Raincliffe Woods p57

Kirkbymoorside

Dalby Forest (Bridestones) p58

Scarborough

Forge Valley Woods p57

Stables Wood & Roffe Wood p60

Pickering

Helmsley

Duncombe Park p60

Chafer Wood p59

Snainton

Eastfie...

Oswaldkirk

A1...

Hunma...

Malton

Norton

North Grimston

...lington

Langtoft

Chester-le-Street Riverside

Chester-le-Street

Leaving the A1 at Chester-le-Street junction, take the A167 south heading towards Durham. At the first roundabout turn left, you will see the cricket ground on the right, at the next minor roundabout, turn left into Riverside car park. (NZ282510)
50HA (124 ACRES)
Chester-le-Street District Council

Few other northeast sites offer the same mix of historic woodland, architectural features,

Ragpath Wood

modern change, artistic adventure and riverside babble.

Here, in the heart of town, are ornamental gardens, picnic areas and riverside walks in beautiful countryside overlooked by Lumley Castle. It has all you need for a group stroll or long distance adventure – and as part of the Great North Forest there is a huge range of recreational opportunities.

The River Wear, with its thriving birdlife, snakes around the park and the riverside trail leads to a large nature area – a great place to rest and observe.

On the opposite bank, a public right of way runs through the woodland of the Scarborough Estate, where a good mix of deciduous species surround the castle. Access can be difficult, particularly in winter, but the spring flora is worth the effort.

Black Plantation

Lanchester

Take B6296 southwest of Lanchester following signs for Satley. Once over river bridge, wood is on left. Parking for one to two vehicles is available in the lay-by just before the wood.
(NZ136449)
14HA (34 ACRES)
The Woodland Trust

Lying on the south bank of the River Browney, Black Plantation is packed with interest.

Roe deer, foxes, various birds and the uncommon orange underwing moth are among the many wildlife species to be found here.

Dominated by birch with the occasional oak, beech, willow and Scots pine the site was enriched with an oak planting programme in 2001. An opportunity for visitors to see tomorrow's wood in the making.

The western half of the site is wet birch woodland with grasses and ferns beneath. On the east it is much drier. Here you will find a good mix of holly, hazel, guelder rose and bird cherry. Ground cover includes wild strawberry, lesser celandine, dog violet, wood sorrel and common bugle.

A circular route leads through the wood via a network of permissive paths.

Ragpath Wood

Esh Winning

Take B6302 west from Durham to Esh Winning. Park in the village, walk along Station View then left to follow the minor road round onto Woodland Terrace. At the end of Woodland Terrace a bridleway leads into the wood. (NZ199418)

33HA (82 ACRES)

The Woodland Trust

Ragpath Wood is a large mixed woodland set in the Deerness valley. Spread across the steep hillside overlooking the old mining village of Esh Winning, Ragpath forms the eastern end of a plantation belt covering the valley's southern side.

This ancient woodland site was planted in the 1950s with larch, Scots pine, spruce, sycamore and beech, though a scattering of oak and birch still survives.

It is popular, not just with locals but also large numbers from outside the valley since the old railway line sandwiched between the wood and village now forms part of the Deerness Valley Walk.

While the sparse understorey is dominated by holly, much of the steep slopes have a layer of heather, bilberry, gorse and broom. Head for the flatter areas by the river to enjoy carpets of ramsons, wood anemone and wood sorrel. Look too for insectivorous butterbur plants.

Edmondsley Wood

Chester-le-Street

From A167 head for Waldridge Fell and then on to Edmondsley village. Go straight over crossroads and park 300m on right after the allotments. (NZ228494)

13HA (32ACRES)

Durham Wildlife Trust

Elemore Woods

Elemore Woods

Easington Lane
Follow Elemore Lane southwest out of
Easington Lane towards High Pittington.
Park in the hamlet of Elemore Vale and
walk past the public house southwards
and follow the public footpath across
the fields to the wood. (NZ355440)
70HA (174 ACRES)
The Woodland Trust

Set in the heart of a stretch of
arable farmland, Elemore Woods is
a wildlife haven on the Magnesian
limestone plateau southwest of
Easington Lane.

This conifer-dominated site is
dotted with occasional broadleaves
– sycamore, ash, beech and elm
which used to abound before
the site was replanted in the
early 1960s. Wych elm is common,
particularly among the understorey.

The beech areas, in particular, are worth visiting in the
autumn when their leaves take
on wonderfully vibrant hues.

The shrub layer is well
developed in some parts, with hazel
and holly forming dense thickets
and providing an important food
source for small mammals such as
wood mice. Robins, woodpeckers
and wrens may be seen year-
round. In early summer, the
ground flora of dog's mercury, red
campion and columbine, is alive
with humming bees.

An extensive network of
footpaths and tracks weaves
through the site.

Hawthorn Dene

Seaham
Leave A19 at Easington on B1283. Turn
left onto B1432 to Hawthorne village.
Take first right after village. Park at
cottage. (NZ433457)
69HA (170ACRES) SSSI
Durham Wildlife Trust

Durham's second largest coastal
dene, featuring relatively
unspoilt woodland which
clings to the steep sides of a
Magnesian limestone ravine.

Ash, elm and sycamore trees dominate the woodland and mature yews stand out on the steep northern slopes while the woodland floor is carpeted with a colourful spring display of wild garlic, bluebell and snowdrop. Less common species such as early purple orchid, birds nest orchid and herb paris also grow here.

Alert visitors might be lucky to spot a roe deer, fox or badger and the bird population includes jay, treecreeper, green and greater spotted woodpeckers.

Over in the eastern part of the reserve there is an area of grassland where summer visitors – particularly those coming in July and August – can enjoy vast numbers of butterflies drawn by the abundance of ground flora including fairy flax, quaking grass, bloody cranesbill and dyers greenwood.

Castle Eden Dene 🔲

Castle Eden
Follow brown tourist signs on A19 and
from Peterlee. Car park off Durham
Way. (NZ410387)
222HA (549ACRES)
English Nature

"A truly breathtaking journey" – one visitor's description of a walk through this award-winning nature reserve. Set on the northern edge of The Tees

Forest, this wildlife haven forms the northeast's largest area of broadleaf woodland.

The 6.5km (4 miles) expanse of wild ancient woodland runs along a deep, steep gorge where mystic yews emerge from strange rocks. For a thousand years this place has spawned stories, poetry and tales of the Devil.

Exploration is via a 12-mile network of paths and more than 25 footbridges though sturdy footwear is needed on steep, sometimes slippery routes. An eight-mile round trip takes visitors through a tangled mix of yew, oak, ash and dying elms before the crash of waves heralds arrival at the Durham coastline.

The dene features a wealth of wildflowers, 300 different fungi and, with more than 3,000 species, is the northeast's richest sites for insects. In winter you might spot red squirrels or hear tawny owls at night. Less common sights are the roe deer, foxes and badgers.

Low Barns
Nature Reserve 🔲

Witton-le-Wear
Take minor road off A68 through
village of Witton-le-Wear. Look for
brown tourist sign. (NZ163313)
50HA (124ACRES) SSSI
Durham Wildlife Trust

Hamsterley Forest

Bishop Auckland

Follow A689 towards Wolsingham. On nearing Wolsingham turn right towards Chatterley. Continue along minor road (Shull Bank) and turn right just before Bedburn into Redford Lane. Take first left, car park 250m on right.

(NZ092313)

2,500HA (6,179ACRES) SSSI

Forestry Commission

County Durham's largest forest, Hamsterley is also one of its most popular tourist attractions.

There is little surprise at its appeal. Hanging on the edge of the North Pennines Area of Outstanding Natural Beauty, between the Durham Dales and Teesdale, this is a natural wonder.

More than 150,000 visitors arrive every year and yet the tranquillity of this special place is to be savoured. Taking a stroll alongside Low Redford Meadow, an SSSI with more than 100 species of plants, and an array of birdlife including pied flycatchers and nightjars, is a wonderfully calming experience.

This working forest centres on the steep valley of the Ayhope and Bedburn becks and houses a rich and varied collection of habitats. Conifer covers much of the site with some mature Scots pine more than 70 years old. Along Bedburn Beck are areas of mixed and broadleaved woodland including 62 acres of oak woods.

Hamsterley is brimming with wildlife – no wonder acclaimed naturalist David Bellamy made his home nearby! Roe deer and badger feature among the variety of mammals that thrive on this site. The forest is also renowned for its large reptile population and colourful butterflies.

A real treat is the tree walk, where you can find some of the oldest trees in the forest. Planted last century by the Surtees family, mature monkey puzzle, giant redwood and yew stand today alongside a variety of creative sculptures.

A 6.5km (4 miles) forest drive provides access to six waymarked trails and picnic areas so it is easy to explore widely – if you have the time! Those who prefer a brisker pace can take advantage of the full events programme or call at the visitor centre and pick up details of the many walking, cycling, horse riding and orienteering opportunities Hamsterley affords.

Errington Wood

New Marske
From A174 head south to New Marske and Grewgrass Lane, turn left at the top of the hill into picnic area. (NZ618203)
80HA (198ACRES)
Langbaugh on Tees Borough Council

At the heart of The Tees Forest, Errington Wood has drawn man since the Stone Age.

A circular walk around the wood offers the chance to enjoy the sights, sounds and history of the wood – and drink in the contrasting Teesside scenery from the imposing coastline at Saltburn across to Guisborough and the moors.

Bronze Age chieftains were buried here. Later it became a centre for ironstone mining. The wood has been forested for more than 100 years and is popular today with dog owners. Work is underway to enrich its habitats by supplementing the dominant pine, larch and spruce with oak, ash, birch, cherry and beech.

An open grassland area, dotted with gorse, elder, rose and thorn, teems with insect and birdlife. Some 90 bird species have been recorded, along with hedgehogs, stoats, roe deer, foxes and badgers.

A good network of paths

serves the site, which can be enjoyed as part of the Upleatham Hills circular walk.

Guisborough Forest (Hutton Lowcross Woods)

Guisborough
A171 east from Middlesbrough, after 4km on dual carriageway take the A173. Car park is 800m on left after minor road to Guisborough. (NZ585152)
478HA (1,181ACRES) NP
Forestry Commission

Guisborough Forest, gateway to the North York Moors National Park and The Tees Forest, extends a warm welcome to visitors, with excellent access and enviable views over Guisborough and nearby Roseberry Topping.

This prominent local landscape feature is a mixed commercial woodland dominated by Corsican and Scots pine, spruce and larch with pockets of cherry, ash, sycamore and beech.

The Cleveland Way passes through the forest, which is well served with a visitor centre, tracks, bridleways, footpaths, orienteering and mountain bike courses, and provides a full programme of events. If you want to explore further, take a circular walk to the Topping but wear strong boots.

Bold Venture Gill is a regionally important geological site within the forest where the landscape is punctured with rocky outcrops and airshafts from former ironstone mines.

Listen out for the haunting call of a curlew or lapwing, increasing in numbers. You may spot other ground-nesting birds such as snipe or golden plover.

Newton Wood

Newton under Roseberry
Following the A173 turn right into Roseberry Lane near Newton under Roseberry. At the end of this road turn right into Newton Wood. (NZ575126)
8HA (20ACRES) SSSI NP
The National Trust

Sandwiched between the uniquely shaped landmark Roseberry Topping and the village of Newton under Roseberry, is Newton Wood, a year-round canvas of subtly changing greens and browns.

This important broadleaved woodland forms an important piece of a jigsaw of woods, moors, town, countryside and industry in an area rich in wildlife, particularly moorland birds.

Several paths criss-cross the wood which is mainly mature oak with higher pockets of ash and a developing holly under-storey. In the southern corner of the wood is Cliff Rigg Quarry where the sheer face and shale deposits of former workings are gradually being covered in gorse and birch.

Most visitors use the internal paths to create a circular walk through the wood though it is possible to create a linear walk taking in Roseberry Topping and Guisborough or Easby Moor. The Topping summit provides magnificent 360-degree views reaching – on a clear day – across The Tees Forest to Teesside and to the Yorkshire Dales.

Flatts Lane Woodland Country Park

Ormesby
On A171 heading east out of Middlesbrough, either turn left into Flatts Lane at Country Park sign or 1km further on there is a car park on left. (NZ547168)
40HA (99ACRES)
Redcar and Cleveland Borough Council

Rifts Wood

Saltburn

Eastern edge of Saltburn Park at pay
and display, signposted Beach, Valley
Gardens. Follow path along beck
through gardens. (NZ666208)
35HA (87ACRES)
**Redcar and Cleveland
Borough Council**

Interest and surprise wait
around many a corner in Rifts
Wood, a delightful treat on the
eastern edge of The Tees Forest.

Just minutes from the beach
and approached via award-
winning Italian gardens complete
with miniature railway, it is
perfect for restless youngsters.

Walking into the heart of the
wood in spring, you'll catch
the aroma of wild garlic that
carpets the woodland floor –
and you are transported into
a world of tumbling
undergrowth where stately
oak, ash and beech cling to the
valley sides. Below them hazel,
holly and ivy grow and lower
still hart's tongue and broad
buckler ferns enjoy the moist
atmosphere.

Skelton Beck rushes between
ironstone outcrops drawing
dippers, grey wagtails and even
kingfishers. Across the gorge,
the neo-Gothic splendour of
Rushpool Hall can be glimpsed

through the trees.

An elegantly proportioned
brick viaduct provides a
surprising and dramatic feature
and further on are small falls
which are particularly
impressive after rain.

Whitecliff, Rosecroft, Clarkson's and Loftus Woods

Loftus

Woods can be accessed from A174 and
B1366 south of Loftus. (NZ712184)
23HA (57ACRES)
**Redcar and Cleveland
Borough Council**

Though it is not immediately
obvious, there are some
spectacular sights and surprises
in Whitecliff, Rosecroft,
Clarkson's and Loftus Woods.

Here, a feel of lush rainforest
contrasts with the riverbed's
rocky ironstone outcrops. Oak,
ash and alder predominate
above a dense understorey of
holly, thorn and guelder rose.

Providing a backdrop to the
village of Loftus, the woods
are an important link with the
wildwood. Their survival is
due to their steep-sided valley
location, whereas vast upland
areas were cleared for crops or
minerals. There is ample
evidence of the ironstone

mining that thrived at nearby Skinningrove and Liverton.

For a great woodland vista, the viaduct near the northwestern edge of Clarkson's Wood provides magnificent valley views with the woods disappearing into the horizon and Kilton Beck escaping to the North Sea.

Although there are no footpath signs or waymarks, a maze of paths, footbridges, steps and gullies run through the site but they can get very wet.

Calfhall, Round Howe and Billybank Woods

Richmond

Following A1 south take right onto A6108 to Richmond. Through Richmond on Leyburn Road, approx 1.6km (1 mile) outside Richmond on left, car park signposted. From car park follow footbridge over River Swale. (NZ156009)

38HA (94ACRES) SSSI

The National Trust

Whitecliff

Mulgrave Woods

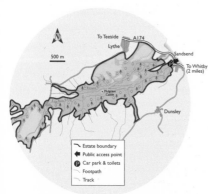

Sandsend

A174 east to Sandsend. Lythe Bank continues into Sandsend Road and wood is on right. (NZ861125) 810HA (2,002ACRES) NP

Marquis of Normanby

Layers of history, myth and legend combine in Mulgrave Woods – a place of year-round magical fantasy.

Even at 2,000 acres, the woodland is an intimate mix of broadleaves – primarily beech, ash, oak and sycamore – and a conifer cocktail of larch, spruce and fir. Cloaking the sides of two valleys, you'll find outlying native oak woods, alder groves mirroring the river's course and a scattering of exotic specimens which add romance.

Mulgrave is a place to be enjoyed at any time of year from spring carpets of snowdrops, bluebells and primroses to the colours of autumn and frosty snowscapes adding a dramatic edge later in the year.

As the landscape climbs from sea level to 260 metres (850ft) areas of open ground allow views within the wood and vistas open up across the distant valley, to Whitby Abbey and out to sea.

Step back in time and discover a Victorian wild garden, an arboretum, traces of a carriage path network and two castles. The more ancient of these survives as a motte in the northwest corner of the wood and although it is hidden from view, is accessible from a public footpath.

The keep of a Norman castle has been carefully preserved, retaining the alterations suggested by the landscape gardener Humphry Repton in 1792. Repton was responsible for many of the features of the woods including a dry arch, stone bridges and the rock tunnel.

The Georgian country house with turrets and battlements added in the early 19th century completes the fantasy.

A continuing programme of selective felling and planting is restoring Repton's vision for the site. Indeed the bulk of the forestry work today involves maintaining and enhancing these landscape features.

Little Beck Wood

Sneaton

8km (5 miles) west of Robin Hood's
Bay. Take B1416 to Littlebeck and park
in village hall car park. Reserve entrance
100m downhill by ford. (NZ880050)
13HA (32ACRES) NP
Yorkshire Wildlife Trust

A tour of this sheltered woodland gem, near the picturesque
hamlet of Littlebeck throws up
many clues and insights into its
past, including a strong industrial heritage and links with the
wildwood.

Nestling in a deeply cut
valley, the wood has a humid
atmosphere allowing fungi and
bryophyte communities to
thrive. Alders overhang stream-
side communities of moschatel,
saxifrage, fleabane and sneeze-
wort while higher up the valley
hazel and holly grow beneath
oak and ash.

Shales, exposed by fallen
trees, provide evidence of the
once all-important 18th-century
quarrying for alum here. In
spring the wood is resplendent
with bluebells, primroses and
early purple orchid.

Little Beck has good links
with nearby Sneaton Forest
and its crowd-pulling Falling
Foss. But remember to wear
stout boots or wellies as the
path can become very muddy.

Sneaton Forest

Whitby

Take A171 north from Scarborough.
Turn left onto B1416 to Sneaton. Turn
sharp left into Foss Lane (not minor
road to Littlebeck) and follow track
downhill to Forestry Commission car
park. (NZ888036) NP
1,209HA (2,988ACRES)
Forestry Commission

The star attraction of Sneaton
Forest, for the visitor at least, is
the Falling Foss, a 10 metre
high waterfall that stages a
particularly spectacular display
after heavy rain.

It lies within the old
broadleaved woodland that lines
steep valleys and makes up the
northern section of the forest.
All can be explored via generally
well surfaced paths, new footbridges and ironstone steps.

From this focal point, a
number of public footpaths
radiate to give access to the
surrounding woods including
the 1960s conifer plantation
that makes up the larger and
southern section of the site.

One of the paths links to
Littlebeck via the Hermitage, a
folly carved from a huge boulder,
and provides fine views across
the surrounding moorland.

Other paths lead out onto
the moors via the May Beck
Picnic Place and into the nearby

Newton House plantation, where the woodland cover changes in character. Here beech is dominant, with pockets of larchwood.

Harry's Folly, Boggle Top & Hone Wood

Ravenscar, Fylingdales
Situated approximately 3km (2 miles) southwest of Robin Hood's Bay, within the North York Moors National Park.
(NZ935015)
16HA (39 ACRES) NP
The Woodland Trust

Less than two miles from the coastal town of Robin Hood's Bay, these adjacent woods form part of a much larger chain of ancient woodland.

Relatively undisturbed, Harry's Folly was extended by the Woodland Trust in 1998 through a woodland creation scheme. It is particularly vibrant during spring and early summer, thanks to successive displays of snowdrops, primroses, bluebells and daffodils. Dominated by oak and ash, the wood has a dense understorey of hazel.

Nearby Boggle Top was created in 2001 with the backing of the local community and planted with native species including oak, ash, rowan, field maple and cherry. Seating provided at the southern end of the wood offers magnificent views across Robin Hood's Bay.

Few outside influences have touched neighbouring Hone Wood, a 9.5-acre oak-dominated ancient woodland rich in plant species. Inaccessible for decades, it can now be accessed via Boggle Top. As no paths have been created, to protect the undisturbed woodland, please tread with care.

Harry's Folly

Scar and Castlebeck

Scar & Castlebeck Woods

Harwood Dale
Follow signs from A171 for Harwood
Dale. (SE946971)
52HA (130 ACRES) SSSI NP
The Woodland Trust

If you have ever wanted to tread in the footsteps of dinosaurs, visit Scar and Castlebeck Woods in the beautiful North York Moors National Park.

The secluded woods straddle a steep ravine carved by the streams and small rivers that run off the moors – among them Castlebeck, Jugger How Beck and Bloody Beck, cited as one of the best inland exposures of dinosaur footprints.

Designated a Site of special Scientific Interest, it is home to 23 nationally scarce insects and the most northeasterly place to find the brimstone butterfly.

Trout, kingfisher and heron abound in the river while the woods are home to many bird species including owl, woodpecker, woodcock and pied flycatcher.

A wealth of mosses and liverworts flourish on the damp valley sides while ferns and grasses thrive on the moderately acidic soils. Scar Wood also boasts some of Britain's largest examples of rare hay-scented buckler fern.

A public footpath provides good access but wellingtons are recommended.

Forge Valley Woods

Scarborough

Turn north off the A170 at East Ayton
and follow road next to river. Wood is
on either side of river. (SE985865)
95HA (235ACRES) SSSI NP
Scarborough Borough Council

Woods have been present in
the Forge Valley for 6,000
years. This tranquil, mixed
deciduous woodland preserves
an ancient link with the wildwood.

The origins of the Ice Age
valley's name dates back to the
14th century when charcoal
was produced for local forges.

A walk along the Derwent
river – where grayling, trout
and crayfish thrive – leads
through alder groves. Higher
up the valley oak is more
prominent, with a dense
understorey of hazel and holly.

The rock is exposed in
dramatic sheer faces. Petrifying
springs in Scarwell Wood
illustrate the eerie effect of the
limestone deposits.

The woodland sustains a
variety of birds from grey wagtail
and kingfisher to tree creeper
and siskin. Flag iris, dog's
mercury and primrose add
floral interest.

Paths are well surfaced with
varied walks.

Raincliffe Woods

Scarborough

Follow A171 north out of Scarborough.
By Yorkshire Coast College turn left
into Lady Edith's Drive. Wood is
located 1km (0.75 mile) along the road
on the left hand side. (SE995885)
150HA (371ACRES) SSSI NP
Scarborough Borough Council

Hayburn Wyke

Scarborough

Take A171 north from Scarborough.
Turn right at Cloughton onto minor
road signposted Ravenscar. Wood is
2km on right behind Hayburn Wyke
Hotel. (TA010970) NP
The National Trust

Broxa Forest

Burniston

At Burniston on A171 turn west signed
Harwood Dale. After 200m turn left
(for Suffield). At the junction at top of
hill (2km), turn right. After 2km forest
lies on either side of road. (SE965945)
733HA (1812ACRES) NP
Forestry Commission

Levisham Wood

Levisham

Pickering

Follow A169 north from Pickering for approximately 9km (5.5 miles). Turn left into Lockton village. Follow minor road to Levisham. Turn left at top of village and along to south end of Little Field Lane. Continue along bridleway to enter wood. (SE826896)

64HA (158ACRES) NP

North York Moors
National Park Authority

Step back into the golden age of steam. For steam train is the best way to approach Newtondale, one of the most spectacular valleys in Yorkshire, where George Stephenson's famous line still echoes to their romantic breath and whistle.

The train provides some of the most spectacular views of the steep-sided valley with its magnificent and rugged scenery, picturesque villages and swathes of woodland, Levisham Wood being part of a wider woodland complex.

Much of the valley's original woodland cover – oak, ash, birch and lime – has survived. The occasional clutch of conifers add a dash of texture and colour to the bare broadleaf outlines in winter and there is a dense understorey of hazel, holly and hawthorn.

Use the extensive network of paths to explore remote corners.

Dalby Forest (Bridestones)

Pickering

From Scarborough turn north off A170 at Thortnon-le-Dale. After 3km (2 miles) turn right into forest drive. (SE857874)

3598HA (8893ACRES) NP

Forestry Commission

Adorning a landscape shaped by the Ice Age, Dalby Forest is a vast man-made creation that provides the visitor with a memorable experience that is unique in Britain.

The ancient forest now gone, the site on the southern slopes of the North York Moors National Park has evolved into a hugely popular recreational venue and wildlife haven.

But a cruise along the nine mile Dalby Forest Drive – one of a network of excellent forest roads – is a drive down the road of time and a virtual geology field trip through the Jurassic period. Burial mounds, linear earthworks and the remains of a once-flourishing rabbit warren industry dot the forest.

Apart from pockets of deciduous woodland, where primrose and meadowsweet grow, conifers dominate the forest replanted as a timber resource from the 1920s. It is home to various birds such as the crossbill, nightjar and harrier, while mammals such as deer and badger also abound.

Chafer Wood ▢

Ebberston

Turn right off A170 from Scarborough, just north of Ebberston village. Wood is 200m up minor road on left. (SE899832) 30HA (74ACRES)

Yorkshire Wildlife Trust

Small is beautiful – as Chafer Wood proves. Though not as vast as nearby Dalby Forest, this is a gem of a wood, intimate and packed with year-round interest.

There is an entrance to the wood near a recently restored walled area known as the Pinfold and King Alfred's cairn, site of a natural cave that was used as a burial chamber in Neolithic times with its own romantic legend.

A steep climb along a well-surfaced path provides magnificent views across the Vale of Pickering. En route, the wood's character unfolds, the slopes covered with ash, cherry and blackthorn.

Work to clear thorn and bracken is already producing an abundance of lime-loving plants including cowslip, salad burnet and pyramidal orchids. Spring brings carpets of bluebells and wood anemones.

The circular walk descends to the road via Netherby Dale dykes and returns along the valley bottom with its marsh orchids, marigolds and gypsywort.

Stables Wood & Roffe Wood

Sinnington

Off the A170 to the west of Pickering. Limited parking available in the village only. (SE748863/SE750862)

8HA (20 ACRES)

The Woodland Trust

Stables Wood has had no public access in living memory. However, work by the Woodland Trust to create a neighbouring native broadleaf wood has now opened this up.

Roffe Wood, planted as part of the Trust's millennium 'Woods on your Doorstep' project, is a small community-designed site that is already well used by local people.

A permissive path circling the site continues through Stables Wood, an ancient woodland remnant sitting on a gentle south-facing slope. This provides a reminder of what surrounding agricultural land may once have looked like.

Dominated by oak, there is hazel coppice, holly, field maple, dog rose, hawthorn and blackthorn beneath. The rich ground flora is notable for dog's mercury, bluebells, grasses and mosses.

Stables Wood forms part of a broken chain of woodland that follows the river valley and finally links with the Forestry Commission's vast Cropton Forest.

Duncombe Park

Helmsley

Heading north on A1(M) turn off at J49, onto A168. Turn right onto A170. Take left off this road toward Duncombe Park. Signposted in Helmsley. (SE603832)

165HA (408ACRES) AONB SSSI NP

Helmsley Estate

Overlooking medieval Helmsley Castle and the River Rye valley, the estate is made up of an impressive early 18th-century house set in 35 acres of landscaped gardens surrounded by 400 acres of parkland. Half the parkland is a designated National Nature Reserve.

The reserve includes remnants of ancient woodland and provides a sanctuary for some of England's oldest and tallest trees, distinguished by their elegantly gnarled and decaying limbs.

A well-signed river walk offers fine views across to Helmsley and the moors as the route follows the curve of the river through Terrace Bank Woods.

Although access is restricted to opening hours, the Cleveland Way takes in some of the estate's new coniferous plantations.

Garbutt Wood

Garbutt Wood

Thirlby

Park at Sutton Bank National Park
Centre, 9.5km (6 miles) east of Thirsk,
and follow Cleveland Way north. Take
sloping path down escarpment at nature
trail sign. (SE505835)
24HA (59ACRES) SSSI NP
Yorkshire Wildlife Trust

There is a mystery to Garbutt
Wood, where gnarled and
twisted veteran oaks and birches
lend a 'Tolkeinesque' quality.

This atmospheric site is part
of the Sutton Bank National
Park Centre.

Superb views open up
almost as soon as you enter
and a well marked nature trail
leads through open bracken
areas, dotted with birch and
mature oak and alive with
bluebells in spring. In denser
woodland pockets oak, birch,
ash, rowan, hazel, holly and
hawthorn are supplemented
with crab apple, willow and
alder that grow by the springs
that emerge from the rocks.

It is worth visiting the
national park's only natural lake
– moody Gormire lake – to
catch a glimpse of waterfowl or
mini forests of water horsetail.

Heading back towards the
Cleveland Way through dew-
drenched bilberry and heather,
you encounter the sheer face of
Whitestone Cliff.

Hambleton Woods

Thirlby

A170 east from Thirsk to Sutton Bank.
Wood to east of car park. (SE515830)
174HA (430ACRES) NP
Tillhill Forestry

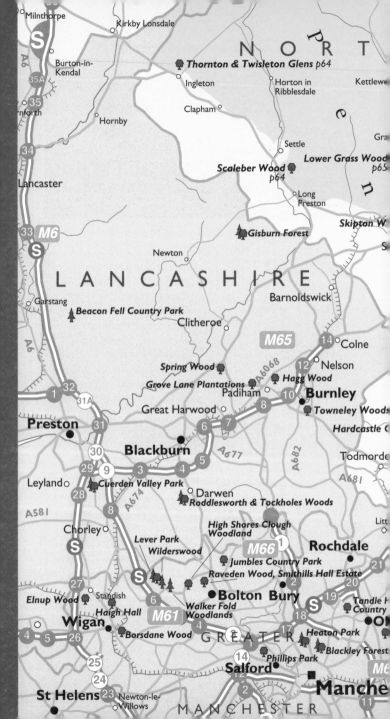

YORKSHIRE

🌳 *Hackfall p66*

Topcliffe

Ripon

Easingw

Pateley
Bridge

Boroughbridge

Ouse

A1(M)

Ripley

Knaresborough

🌳 *Strid Wood p68*

🌲 *Swinsty
Reservoir
p71*

Harrogate

Spofforth

Nidd

Wetherby

Boston Spa

A659

🌲 *Middleton Wood p69*

Ilkley

Otley

🌲 *Harewood p70*

A659

Ta

Steeton

🌲 *Chevin Forest Park p70*

A1

Keighley

🌳 *Park Wood p73*

Ⓐ *Leeds Bradford Int.*

Bingley

🌲 *Elsholt Woods p71*

St Ives Estate
p72

🌲 *Hirst Wood p73*

Leeds

48

47

🌳 *Northcliffe Wood p73*

46

Garforth

45

Bradford

Pudsey

1

47

45

Queensbury

43

44

Halifax

🌲 *Judy Woods p74*

27

28

42

30

Castlefor

26

31

32

33

W E S T   S

Y O R K   S

H I R E

S

Pontefr

25

Dewsbury

41

24

40

Wakefield

23

A58

Huddersfield

39

🌲 *Stoneycliffe Wood p75*

S

South
Kirkby

A640

S

Holmfirth

A635

A616

A6024

M1

37

Barnsley

Wombwell

🌲 *Bagger Wood p76*

Mexbor

36

Strinesdale
Countryside
Area

S O U T H   Y O R K S H I R

Glossop

Chapeltown

35

Rotherham

Thornton & Twisleton Glens

Ingleton

On the edge of Ingleton village parking is provided for the Waterfalls Walk (signposted) by the Ingleton Scenery company, which charges for parking and access.

(SD695750/SD700742)

8HA (20 ACRES) SSSI NP

The Woodland Trust

Ancient woodland is something of a rarity in North Yorkshire making Thornton and Twisleton Glens all the more valuable.

Situated on the banks of the River Twiss and River Doe, the two woods are part of a larger unbroken chain of ancient woodland following each river's course in the Yorkshire Dales National Park.

Both woods are accessed via the stunningly beautiful 7km (4.5 miles) Waterfalls Walk from Ingleton. Since the late 19th century, visitors have enjoyed this route which includes ancient oak woodland, geological features and magnificent Dales scenery.

The walk leads you through spectacular landscapes of dramatic outcrops with cascades and waterfalls – the most famous being Thornton Force. There is a viewing area here where you can enjoy a picnic and watch the river fall 14 metres over limestone rocks in an impressive cascade. Also, don't miss Snow Falls beside Twisleton Glen. Look for lichens and soft mosses that thrive in the deep dark gullies.

Scaleber Wood

Settle

From Settle follow High Hill Lane southeast. A small area for parking directly adjacent to wood. (SD840625)

4HA (10 ACRES) SSSI NP

The Woodland Trust

A real people magnet, Scaleber Wood in the heart of the Yorkshire Dales packs a power-ful mix of breathtaking sights and evocative sounds into a small space.

The most spectacular is Scaleber Force, a stunning 40ft waterfall whose crystal waters tumble over limestone cliffs before plunging into a deep pool.

The site lies on the Elgar Way – named after the great English composer who was a regular visitor – a 21km (13 mile) circular walk from Settle that takes in impressive crags, gorges and waterfalls.

Scaleber Wood lies within the Attermire Scar, site of special scientific interest for its remarkable limestone geology with huge limestone outcrops and the associated flora.

The wood itself, a mix of broadleaves and planted conifers is tricky to access and taxing to explore, but only a short walk from the road is needed to reveal the spectacular sight of the waterfall from a viewpoint.

Lower Grass Wood

Grassington
From Grassington follow Grass Wood Lane north and park where there are a number of lay-bys and a small, Yorkshire Wildlife Trust car park. (SD983651)
8.5HA (21 ACRES) NP
The Woodland Trust

Ancient woodland adorns this stretch of the River Wharfe valley less than a mile from Grassington.

This linear broadleaf site is an important part of one of the Yorkshire Dales National Park's largest ancient woodland areas.

The wood has an open character, due to the loss of most elm trees, with a light canopy of sycamore, oak, ash and birch. But Nature is plugging the gaps with dense patches of regenerating hawthorn, birch, beech and ash.

A wealth of colourful flowers includes carpets of bluebells and dog's mercury, orchids during summer and rich carpets of herbs on the steep open riverside slopes. Two 'elling hearths', small stone-lined pits used to produce potash, can be seen here.

Extend your visit by crossing the road to Yorkshire Wildlife Trust's Grass Wood and climb toward open ground at its summit. An extensive programme of restoration work is returning this wood to its former glory.

Lower Grass Wood

Hackfall

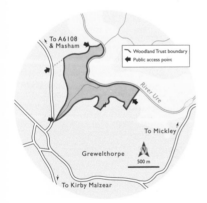

Grewelthorpe

Follow A6108 north of Ripon. Take first left after North Stainley through Mickley, and right at T-junction to Grewelthorpe. Wood is situated on the edge of Grewelthorpe, on the road towards Masham. Park in Grewelthorpe and walk 200m on road toward Masham, entrance to wood on right. (SE236771)

45HA (110 ACRES) AONB, SSSI
The Woodland Trust

There is something about the wild splendour of Hackfall Woods that simply inspires creativity (see additional photo on p77). Nineteenth-century writers hailed it as one of the most beautiful woodlands in the country while romantic landscape artist Turner painted in the woods.

Set in a 350-ft gorge on the edge of Grewelthorpe, the site was bought in 1731 by John Aislabie, famous for his land-scaping work at nearby Fountains Abbey and Studley Royal.

But it was his son, William who transformed the area into a 'beautiful wilderness', creating grottos and surprise views, glades, rustic temples embedded in groves of trees, waterfalls and follies – many of which can still be discovered in the park today.

In its Victorian heyday, visitors flocked to view the woods and house and enjoy teas at Mowbray Point, where the Aislabies had entertained friends.

It is possible that conifers were planted in the 19th century to supplement the largely broadleaved woodland but almost the entire wood was felled during the 1930s and regeneration since then has been at the hands of Nature.

For half a century the site fell into decline but since the 1980s, when the Woodland Trust took over, much has been done to return Hackfall to its former glory, restoring footpaths and woodland walks, conserving the various follies, managing the fragile habitats, and giving Hackfall a future.

Part of the area is designated a Site of Special Scientific Interest. The largely broadleaved woodland is still dominated by oak with beech, sycamore, ash and even lime originating from the 18th century.

Modern visitors can once again bask in the stunning scenery and enjoy period features including a host of man-made waterfalls and water courses displayed throughout the woodland.

Hackfall teems with wildlife and sustains a thriving range of wild plant communities including a spectacular display of bluebells.

Strid Wood

Bolton Abbey

From A59 turn onto B6160 following
signs for Bolton Abbey. Continue north
for approximately 5km (3 miles) to Strid
car park on right. (SE058563)
46HA (114ACRES) SSSI NP
**Trustees of the Chatsworth
Settlement – Yorkshire Estate**

Strid Wood has been a popular
destination for almost two
centuries and it is not surprising,
for this is a woodland for all
seasons.

Set along the valley of the
River Wharfe, it forms part of
the Bolton Abbey Estate and
was first opened to visitors in
1810. William Wordsworth

enjoyed the views on frequent
walks through the woods.

The unpolluted waters of the
river gush through the narrow
gorge and support brown trout,
grayling and the uncommon
crayfish while 50 bird species
nest in the area. In summer
dragonflies fly over the water
and in winter, ducks roost on
the banks.

Although this is an ancient
woodland site, much of the
valley has been replanted with
beech, sycamore, larch and
spruce. But large areas of
sessile oak provides a valuable
habitat for a variety of wildlife
including rare flowering plants,
fungi and lichens.

Whilst exploring Bolton
Abbey you may like to follow
the Priory Trail to visit
Wandsworth Wood.

Skipton

Skipton Woods

Skipton
From Skipton town centre car park at
rear of town hall (pay and display)
follow Springs Canal towpath to woods
main entrance. (SD990525)
15HA (37 ACRES)
The Woodland Trust

A magical land in the heart of
town. A woodland haven by
one of Britain's best preserved,
most popular medieval castles.

The wood's links with the
castle date back at least 1,000
years. A canal towpath,
following the line of Skipton
Castle ramparts and Springs
Canal, provides a direct link
between the town's High Street
and the woods, following the
course of Eller Beck through a
stunning steep-sided valley.

Most of this ancient
woodland is dominated by ash
with the occasional sycamore,
beech, Scots pine, Norway
spruce and hornbeam. The
woods are renowned for their
vivid displays of bluebells and
wild garlic and sustain five
species of bat. Kingfisher and
heron may be seen fishing the
waterways.

In 1998, many of the paths
were resurfaced.

Middleton Wood

Ilkley
Follow A65 south to Ilkley. Turn into
New Brook Street at crossroads in
Ilkley and continue up Middleton
Avenue and park on roadside on Curly
Hill. (SE120488)
45HA (111ACRES)
Bradford Metropolitan Council

These mixed broadleaved
amenity woods grow on
terraces created by gritstone
outcrops on the hills above
Ilkley and feature a stunning
display of bluebells.

Small streams cascading
down the hillside over rocky
ledges and mossy boulders are
bordered by damp areas where
large alders grow.

A good network of footpaths
links the open country above
the wood where you can enjoy
wonderful views.

The woodland east of the
road is a delightful site with
much to explore. An abun-
dance of dead timber provides
a rich habitat for small birds
and insects. There are good
paths here too and occasional
benches where you can stop to
enjoy the woodland scene.

Harewood

Harrogate

The village of Harewood is centrally
placed in Yorkshire at the junction of
the A61/A659 on the Leeds/Harrogate
road. (SE312446)
55HA (136 ACRES)
Harewood House Trust

Visitors flock in their
thousands to enjoy the sights
and sounds of Harewood
House and grounds, winner of
Yorkshire Tourist Board's 2002
Visitor Attraction of the Year
award.

Open to the public from
March to October, the house
and grounds includes acres of
beautiful parkland with trees
and mainly broadleaved copses
as well as extensive boundary
plantations.

Around the lake is a large
area of historic amenity woodland, created by Capability
Brown and these areas are
managed carefully to preserve
the site's landscape heritage.

Visitors can enjoy any
number of charming walks
through dappled and shaded
woods, where the ground is
covered in spring bulbs,
rhododendron and unusual
shrubs.

Chevin Forest Park

Otley

A660 through Otley, following signs to
The Chevin. (SE225445)
168HA (415ACRES) SSSI
Leeds City Council

Chevin Forest Park was
created for and donated to the
residents of Otley as a living
memorial to those who gave
their lives during World War II.

Today it is a testament to peace
and forms part of the Forest of
Leeds where wildlife, including
a plethora of birds thrives.

The woods clothe the steep
gritstone escarpment that
dominates Otley. Varied and
interesting, they include areas
of ancient woodland with
plantations of conifers and
mixed broadleaves.

Heather and bilberry grow
on the open landscape set
above the wood but below the
top of the ridge. The green
hairstreak butterfly breeds in
the gorse scrub while wetter
sections support bog asphodel.

There is a good network of
walks throughout the area and
visitors of all ages and abilities
can plan a route that offers variety
and attractive scenery. It is
possible to walk along the ridge
– the reward is magnificent
views across every direction.

Chevin Forest Park

Esholt Woods

Esholt

A6038 (Hollins Hill) north of Shipley.
Turn right into Station Road, just after
Hollins Hall Hotel on opposite side of
road. Car park and wood just after
railway viaduct on left. (SE182404)
75HA (185ACRES)
Bradford Metropolitan Council

Swinsty Reservoir

Fewston

Take A59 (Skipton Road) east, turn
right near Fewston into Cobby Syke
Road. Continue to junction near church
and turn left to Stack Point car park or
turn right and across dam to Swinsty
Moor car park. (SE197538)
200HA (494ACRES)
Yorkshire Water

Additional woods to visit

**Woods shown on the western edge
of map 3 (pp62-63) feature in**
*Exploring Woodland Guide to
Northwest England*. **These include:**

Cuerden Valley Park
Phillips Park
Beacon Fell Country Park
Spring Wood
Strinesdale Countryside Area
Tandle Hill Country Park
Elnup Wood
Haigh Hall
Heaton Park
Grove Lane Plantations
Lever Park
Roddlesworth & Tockholes Woods
Blackley Forest
High Shores Clough Woodland
Jumbles Country Park
Raveden Wood, Smithills Hall Estate
Walker Fold Woodlands
Wilderswood
Gisburn Forest
Borsdane Wood
Hagg Wood

St Ives Estate

Harden

Follow A650 north near to Bingley.
Turn left onto Harden Road (B6429).
Take right through gate posts signed St
Ives Estate. Continue up drive to car
park on right. (SE090390)
81HA (200ACRES)
Bradford Metropolitan Council

The St Ives Estate has been
making its mark on English
history for centuries – and
continues to do so.

Once the home of the
crusading monks of the
Knights Hospitallers and Knights
Templar, it is still contributing
to local heritage. You can still
see the site of the Ferrands Oak,
a massive 12.5-ton specimen
that grew here for 250 years. It
was felled in 1985 and used in
the new south transept of York
Minster.

There are other lovely old
trees at St Ives including a
spreading purple beech near
the car park and the remains of
old sweet chestnut further
down the drive.

Once oak and birch
woodland and heather
moorland, the woods have
been replanted with conifers,
broadleaf and mixed species
with rhododendrons and lots
of specimen trees including
wellingtonia, red oak, Bhutan
pine and London plane.

There are several waymarked
walks.

St Ives Estate

Hirst Wood

Saltaire

Taking A650 south of Bingley, turn left at roundabout where A657 joins A650 into Clarence Road (leading to Hirst Lane). Cross railway line. Car park and wood on left. (SE132382)

15HA (37ACRES)

Bradford Metropolitan Council

Hirst Wood is something of an island, separated from surrounding industrial, residential and agricultural landscapes by a perimeter railway line, river and canal.

Perhaps that is why this attractive wood is so popular with local people.

Predominantly oak and birch, it also has areas of planted beech that add a further dimension to your walk as it rises out of the valley of the River Aire. In the south-west corner of the wood the land slopes steeply down to the fast-flowing river – so take special care.

Holly is plentiful among a ground layer of brambles and bracken but the site is easy to navigate via a number of clearly marked footpaths, some of which link to others through the valley. A surfaced path from the car park provides access for wheelchair users. Elsewhere, paths are prone to mud – so remember your boots.

Park Wood

Keighley

From A650 at Crossflatts follow by-pass. Turn off at roundabout to Thwaites and Worth village. Take first left and cross railway bridge. Follow road into Parkwood Street. Wood is on hillside above Parkwood Street. (SE069409)

14HA (35ACRES)

Bradford Metropolitan Council

Northcliffe Wood

Shipley

From A650 Bradford–Keighley Road take left turn at Frizinghall to Cliff Wood Avenue. The wood is straight ahead. (SE142362)

17HA (42ACRES)

Bradford Metropolitan Council

Hardcastle Crags

Hebden Bridge
Take A6033 (Keighley Road) north of
Hebden Bridge. Turn left into
Midgehole Road, follow to the end into
National Trust car park. (SD988295)
125HA (309ACRES)
The National Trust

A dramatic landscape and
interesting history join forces
at Hardcastle Crags to forge an
attractive woodland of interest
to all ages.

Over the years the steep
wooded valley of Hebden
Gorge has supported a range of
industries – wool from local
farms supplied the mill in the
valley while charcoal burners
provided fuel for local iron
smelting.

Today the steep-sided gorge
is clothed in beech, sycamore,
oak, birch, larch and Scots
pine, planted over 150 years.
Woodrush, ferns, bracken and
bluebells cover the ground
where thousands of wood ants
rustle through the foliage.

Look out for the slurring
stone – a large rock where local
children used to slide in their
clogs, and an old pannier route
which winds up the hillside.

A choice of walks include
the chance to climb the hillside
towards Harcastle Crags, the
rocky outcrops that give the
woods their name. Boots are
recommended, particularly for
anyone venturing onto the
open moors.

Judy Woods

Wyke
From A461 take turning to Norwood
Green. Woodland on left, off Station
Road. (SE137270)
40HA (99ACRES)
Bradford Metropolitan Council

There is a delightfully rural feel
to Judy Woods, a collection of
small sites forming an intimate
patchwork along the valley of
Royds Hall Beck.

The woods sit within a
lovely landscape and look
more extensive than they are.

They also have a rich social
history. Named after Judy
North, who lived in a 19th-
century cottage near the bridge,
they are made up of mixed
broadleaves. Ancient woodland
was replanted with beech in
Victorian times, probably to
serve the local mills. Bell pits
are lasting reminders of the area's
industrial heritage, particularly
in Old Hanna Wood.

The beech, stunning in
spring and autumn, include
some lovely large spreading
specimens along with oak and

birch areas. Small tributaries of the beck add to the variety and higher ground provides lovely views beneath the canopy.

There are lots of paths and potential circular walks, including a surfaced path suitable for wheelchairs and pushchairs.

Stoneycliffe Wood

Netherton
On the B6117 southwest of Wakefield, west of village of Netherton.
(SE274161)
40HA (99ACRES)
Yorkshire Wildlife Trust

Hardcastle Crags

There is an air of peace about Stoneycliffe Wood and a host of interesting features inside.

The woodland clothes the steep slope down to Stoneycliffe Beck which meanders tortuously along the valley. Less athletic visitors can take advantage of benches provided at intervals throughout the wood.

Amid this quiet scene a population of birds thrives – woodpeckers and summer warblers among them – with several rare spider species, while a small pond supports ducks and other wildfowl.

Oak and birch dominate this typical coal measure woodland though sycamore has taken hold in some areas and lovely gnarled and twisted oak and sweet chestnut specimens add to the atmosphere.

Holly, hazel and heather form the understorey with bluebells, ramsons, yellow archangel and several rare plants, including wood club-rush, hemlock water droplet and Sprengels' bramble.

Paths are easy to follow but those along the valley bottom can be muddy and slippery – so boots are recommended.

Bagger Wood

Hood Green

Junction 37 M1 through Dodworth to Silkstone Common on B6449. Turn left in Silkstone Common to Hood Green. Turn right in Hood Green following road for 1.6km (1 mile) before turning right into car park at western end of wood. (SE303026)

27HA (68 ACRES)

The Woodland Trust

Just ten minutes from busy Barnsley, Bagger Wood is a rural haven.

One of a series of steep hillside woods, Bagger and its neighbouring woods form a distinctive skyline, making a particularly attractive landmark from the nearby village of Dodworth and surrounding area.

The wood, which is part of the South Yorkshire Forest, is well placed for access from several local villages. Visitors can either follow an attractive circular path from the car park or explore the central area via a forest road which is also open to horse riders.

Listed as an ancient woodland site, Bagger Wood was dominated by broadleaves until the 1960s when around half was planted with conifers. Most of the hardwoods that remain – oak, beech and sycamore – date from the 1930s.

Towneley Woods

Burnley

Follow signs from M65 and A671 for Towneley Hall Park. (SD855307)

20HA (49ACRES)

Burnley Borough Council

Woodland has existed in the grounds of historic Towneley Hall since 1400 but the visitor's route is along paths laid out in the 1800s when the grounds were landscaped in classic English style.

The legacy of this historical background can be enjoyed among the mixed native broadleaves and exotic species that populate the site today. Look for sculptures created along the walks here and at nearby Grove Lane Plantations, Padiham and in the woods of Gawthorpe Hall.

Many surprises await being discovered including relics from the 19th century such as an arched passageway in Thanet Lee Wood, a ha-ha, rustic tunnels and the Monks Well grotto.

Soil changes throughout the site are reflected in the variety of ground flora – clay-loving ramson in some sections contrasting with an abundance of bluebells in more acidic areas.

Hackfall

NORTH YORKSHIRE

Topcliffe

South Wood p86

Ne

Easingwold

North G

Boroughbridge

Ouse

Stillington

A1(M)

Marton Wood p87

Haxby

Knaresborough

Nidd Gorge p84

Nidd

York

Pockli

Spofforth

Fulford

Allertho
Wood p

Wetherby

YORK

Ha

Boston Spa

A659

New Covert
Park Woods

Ox Close p83

Tadcaster

Holme-o
Spalding-Mo

Hetchell Wood p83

A162

Derwent

Bubwith

A16

A1

48
47

Bishop Wood p82

46 Garforth

Selby

45 Temple Newsam Estate p82

43 44

WEST

A645

37

42 30

Castleford

Knottingley

36

Goole

31 32

33   34

Snaith

35

A

YORKSHIRE

Pontefract

A645

A614

Wakefield

39 Newmillerdam Country Park p81

Haw Park Wood p80

M18 Thorne

Seckar Woods p80

5   1

Notton Woods p81

South
Kirkby

38

Hatfield

C

37 Barnsley

37

Bentley

4

Epw

Wombwell

Doncaster

A161

Mexborough

36

36

2 35 3

A614

SOUTH YORKSHIRE

35

M18

Rotherham

1

Hunmanby

Bempton
Flamborough
Flamborough Head

Langtoft

Bridlington

Bridlington
Bay

ridaythorpe

Great Driffield

Skipsea

Bainton

EAST RIDING

Hornsea

Brandesburton
Leven

OF YORKSHIRE

Market
Weighton

A164

South Skirlaugh

Aldbrough

A1034

Beverley

**CITY OF
KINGSTON
UPON HULL**

North Cave

Holderness

38

🌳 *Little Wold Plantation p89*

Bilton

South Cave

🌳 *Nut Wood, Wauldby Scrogs & Constantine
Wood p88*

Withers

Anlaby

■ **Kingston upon Hull**

A1033

Patringto

Trent

Barton-
upon-Humber

A1077

NORTH

Winterton

A1077

Immingham

**NORTH EAST
LINCOLNSHIRE**

LINCOLNSHIRE

● **Scunthorpe**

Humberside
Int.

✈

5

Grimsby ●

Bottesford

Cleethorpes

M180

4

Brigg

A1084

A1173

Laceby

Tetn

Laughton Forest p89

Caistor

Blyton

Binbrook

Yorkshire Wolds

Seckar Woods

Newmillerdam
Car park signposted from A61 Barnsley
to Wakefield. Turn down Seckar Lane.
(SE326143)
48HA (119ACRES) SSSI
Wakefield Metropolitan District Council

One of only five sites
designated of special scientific
interest in Wakefield, Seckar
Wood is a delightful place to
visit, with lots of variety and
several interesting habitats.

A 'must' for any visitor to
Newmillerdam Country Park,

neighbouring Seckar Wood is a
local nature reserve with
woodland, wet and dry heath
and some rare plants.

Within the woods are the
remains of a summerhouse and
a series of ponds – part of a
never-to-be-completed
landscape plan by photographer
Warner Gothard who bought
the wood in the 1920s.

Modern day owners
Wakefield Metropolitan
District Council recently opened
up areas of water to attract
amphibians and dragonflies
and these support a thriving
colony of horsetails.

Thin soils that developed over
the bare sandstone left from
former mine workings now
support gorse, heather and
wavy hair grass that has created
a distinctive habitat and open
landscape – an attractive contrast
with the rather dense woodland.

Haw Park Wood

Wintersett
A638 heading south, turn right
signposted to Crofton opposite Crofton
Arms public house. Follow tourist signs
to Wintersett village. After Anglers
Retreat public house, turn right. Car
park is 800m on right. (SE375154)
65HA (161ACRES)
Wakefield Metropolitan District Council

Seckar Woods

Newmillerdam Country Park

Newmillerdam
Follow A61 south to Newmillerdam.
Follow brown tourist sign to
Newmillerdam Country Park.
(SE331157)
95HA (235ACRES)
Wakefield Metropolitan District Council

Once part of the Pilkington
family's Chevet Estate,
Newmillerdam Country Park
is a lovely combination of lake
and peaceful broadleaved
woodland.

For many, the lake is the
main attraction. There is a
causeway across the water and
a well surfaced path follows a
circular route around the lake –
providing easy access for
wheelchairs and pushchairs.

The route offers plenty of
interest, from the chance to
view wildfowl on the lake to
exploration of the woods of
oak, sweet chestnut and some
fine mature beech. They are
populated by a plethora of
birdlife – tree creepers, woodpeckers and owls included.

The woods south and west
of the lake are the quieter parts
of the country park. Stands of
pine and larch, planted in the
1950s, are being thinned to
make way for oak, ash, birch
and hazel which will encourage
more wildlife. Bluebells grow
in the southern woodland.

It is worth combining a visit
here with neighbouring Seckar
Wood.

Notton Woods

Notton
Turn off A61 onto B6428 to Royston
(Lee Lane). Notton Wood is on left.
(SE344111)
48HA (119ACRES)
Wakefield Metropolitan District Council

Newmillerdam Country Park

Bishop Wood

Cawood

5km (3 miles) west of Selby and 5km south
of Cawood. On B1222 midway between
Sherburn and Cawood. (SE561333)
330HA (816ACRES)
Forestry Commission

A former ancient woodland
oasis in an agriculture-
dominated landscape, Bishop
Wood creates an immediate
impression of size.

It is easy to get the idea this
is a relatively new wood,
thanks to an extensive post-
war planting programme by
the Forestry Commission.
Scots and Corsican pine,
spruce and poplar are regularly
harvested and replanted.

Native wet woodland species
including alder, willow, birch and
hazel are colonising along the
many streams that line the site.
Dotted about the main woodland
are small groups of mature oak
and ash. In the southern part of
the wood, a sensitive programme
of work is under way to re-
establish native species such as
oak, ash, hazel, alder and birch.

Access is via a range of routes
but since there is no waymarking,
it is worth taking a map and
compass. There are ample
stone rides, enabling less-abled
access but the minor paths off
the main grid can be muddy.

Temple Newsam Estate

Whitkirk

M1 J64. Follow Selby Road A63 west
towards Leeds. Turn left into Colton
Road. Continue along this road, turning
right into The Elm Walk. Wood is on
left. (SE360320)
157HA (388ACRES)
Leeds City Council

Dubbed 'the Hampton Court
of the North', Temple Newsam
Estate has the makings of a
great family day out, whatever
the weather.

Just minutes from Leeds,
this is a country park with
knobs on – a combination of
formal gardens, lakeside and
riverside walks, secluded spots
and masses of public space to
enjoy football, athletics, golf
and play facilities. There is also
a working farm, museum and
rare breeds centre.

Mostly planted in the early
eighteenth century, large areas
were used as deer park and today
form part of the Forest of Leeds.

The name reveals the origins
of the estate, which was granted
to the Knights Templar in 1155.
Capability Brown's influence
can be seen in mature areas of
woodland such as Avenue Woods.
The estate's deserted medieval
village of Colton features veteran
oaks dating back 600 years or more.

Temple Newsam

Hetchell Wood

Thorner

Approaching from Wetherby on A58, at East Rigton turn left signposted Thorner. Keep left at triangular intersection (Milner Lane). Reserve entrance on left after 800m. (SE380422)
11HA (27ACRES) SSSI
Bramham Estates

Ox Close

East Keswick

At Boston Spa exit on A1 take A659 west. 2km (1.5 miles) after Collingham village, turn left signposted East Keswick, car park at junction. Cross road on foot to bridleway. (SE364459)
14HA (35ACRES)
East Keswick Wildlife Trust

Not the easiest wood to find but Ox Close is worth a little effort. For this site – popular with local residents – has much of interest to keep visitors intrigued.

Standing on the edge of the River Wharfe valley, Ox Close Wood is explored via a meandering circular path.

The most accessible areas were cleared 11 years ago but vigorous regeneration of ash, elm, birch and sycamore has left the area rich and dense. Look out for occasional mature larch and pine.

Further along the path, sycamore is more common and scrub is being removed to make way for limestone grassland, encouraged by grazing Hebridean Sheep and the occasional goat. This is a working wood – with two kilns producing charcoal and adding another layer of interest. Rest a while on the recently installed woodland seats by the kilns.

On leaving, it is worth pausing on the robust green footbridge over the River Wharfe to enjoy the fine valley views, explore the banks for signs of crayfish, otters, kingfishers, breeding goosanders and grey wagtails or enjoy a picnic.

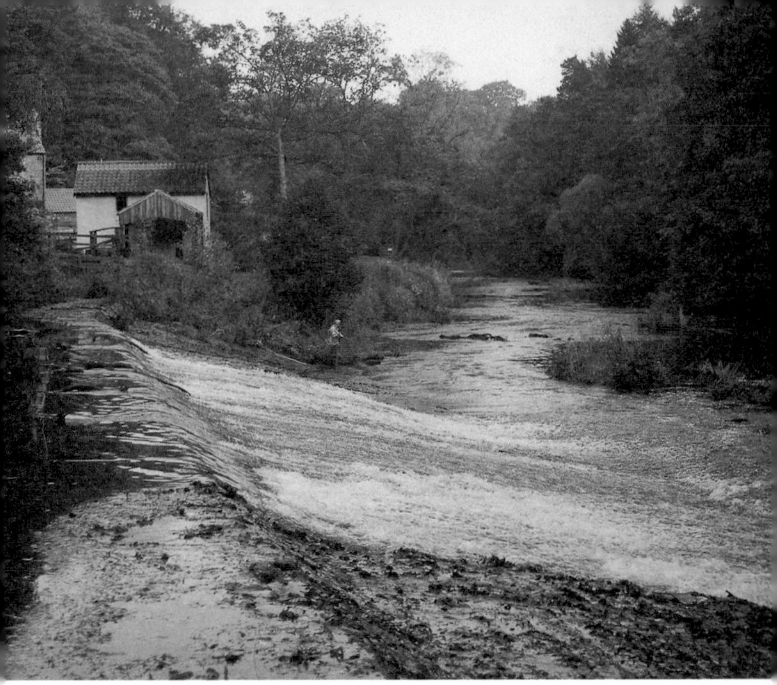

Nidd Gorge

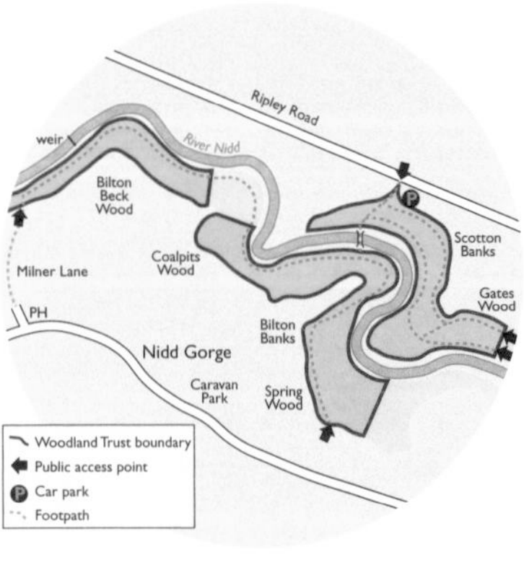
Ripley Road
weir
River Nidd
Bilton Beck Wood
Coalpits Wood
Milner Lane
PH
Scotton Banks
Gates Wood
Bilton Banks
Nidd Gorge
Caravan Park
Spring Wood
Woodland Trust boundary
Public access point
Car park
Footpath

Harrogate

From Knaresborough travel along the B6165 towards Ripley for approx 2km (just over a mile). The road follows alongside a woodland. At the end of the wood take first turning left which leads to a small car park. (SE328579)

45HA (112 ACRES) SSSI

The Woodland Trust

Acres of broadleaf woodland brimming with wildlife adorn the steep cliffs and slopes of Yorkshire's stunning Nidd Gorge.

Nestling between Harrogate and Knaresborough, the woodland, which dates back to at least 1600, is actually made up of five woods, Coalpits Wood, Bilton Banks, Spring Wood, Scotton Banks and Gates Wood.

A local conservation site, the valley woodlands and the surrounding agricultural land are a magnet for local residents, walkers and fishermen. All are drawn to a landscape sculpted by the River Nidd whose waters have rushed around the rocky bends and shallows of this imposing landmark since the last Ice Age when it cut a 120-ft gorge through the soft sandstone.

History has left its mark on Nidd Gorge. At Gates Hill, in the Scotton Banks section of the woodland, now overgrown, is a defensive earthwork where local legend says Colonel Fairfax mounted defence cannon for the siege of Knaresborough during the Civil War. Coalpits Wood, south of the river, retains the remnants of bellpits where coal was once excavated.

Most of the oak woods on the Nidd's southern banks had been cleared by World War II and the area is now dominated by broadleaf coppice regrowth with some regenerating sycamore though the area still has a natural feel to it. The northern bank is a mixture of conifers and mixed broadleaves.

Today the gorge nurtures more than 80 species of birds and 30 different kinds of mammals, reptiles and amphibians. Bats, roe deer, tawny owls, herons and spotted and green woodpeckers are just some of the inhabitants of the five woods.

Ninety-one species of fungi have been identified in the gorge including puffballs, cup fungi, jelly and bracket fungi. There are numerous plants and flowers, which are typically found in ancient woodland, among them nine species of fern, dog's mercury, wild garlic and bluebells.

Bilton Beck & Rudding Bottoms

Knaresborough/Harrogate
Follow directions as for Nidd Gorge.
These woods are an extension of Nidd
Gorge. (SE307583)
17HA (42 ACRES)
The Woodland Trust

South Wood

Hovingham

From Malton take B1257 west. At
Hovingham sign turn left, wood is
1.5km on left. (SE660740)

William Worsley

South Wood at Hovingham
illustrates how serious multi-
purpose forestry can blend
seamlessly with native woodland
and surrounding countryside

The estate takes its forestry
seriously, producing high quality
timber. That is good news for
visitors since it produces an
array of species in various
stages of maturity. It also provides great views across the
surrounding hills.

Spruce, Scots pine, larch,
beech, oak, sweet chestnut and
sycamore make up the woodland
mix, blending harmoniously
with surrounding woods –
Fryton, Wath, Slingsby Banks
and Conesthorpe Bank.

As the woods are used for
sporting activities visitors are
asked to keep to public rights
of way and well-surfaced rides.
Mature oaks feature at key
points in the wood, including
the ridges and there is a
magnificent stand of beech
near the bridleway, which links
a series of earthworks.

The eastern end of South
Wood is bounded by Wath Beck,
where alder and willow provide
dappled shade for wetland
plant and insect communities.

New Covert and Park Woods

Melbourne

From York follow the B1228
(York–Howden) through the villages of
Elvington and Sutton upon Derwent.
Just past the turning to Melbourne
where the road turns south, a car park
can be found approximately 800m from
the junction down a short track approx
20m into wood. (SE732442)

11HA(27 ACRES)

The Woodland Trust

These linked woods provide a
quiet retreat.

Their isolation keeps visitor
numbers low and wildlife
interest high. But the visitor is
well catered for with a car
park, information board and
over one mile of footpaths.

A circular route from the car
park leads through a newly
planted area, past a pond into
New Covert, a wet woodland
dominated by birch with
willow and alder, and into a
clearing – a favourite haunt for
barn owls at twilight. Old
ditches beside the path mark
the wood's boundaries as well
as providing drainage.

New Covert is linked to Park
Wood via a thicket of willow

New Covert

and alder on the edge of a glade, where willow tits can sometimes be heard. Park Wood is precious ancient woodland, dominated by birch where gnarled oak trees provide a haven for wildlife. Volunteers have been installing footbridges, clearing paths and removing rhododendron to give native flowers a chance.

Allerthorpe Wood

Barmby Moor

Head north on A1079 towards Barmby Moor. Take left after turn for Barmby Moor opposite garage into Sutton Lane. Wood is approx 2.5km (1.5 miles) on left. (SE753479)
148HA (366ACRES)
Forestry Commission

If you're looking for a moody, misty place to get to grips with Nature, try a walk around Allerthorpe Wood, particularly in the winter months.

This sheltered wood is popular with local residents, and dog owners in particular, since there are few other local areas of open access land.

There are many walks, including an extensive all-weather surfaced ride network, leading through the plantation. The land is flat, well drained and dominated with Scots pine although the site is fringed with birch and a scattering of oaks. Willow can

also be found in wetter ground.

The open ground has been colonised by gorse, holly and birch. Some areas where conifers have been removed will remain unplanted to allow heather to re-colonise.

The wood's southern boundary abuts the modern stables at Thornton House Farm where a bridleway provides a link through to Allerthorpe. It's also worth combining a visit here with a trip to nearby Weldrake Wood or simply enjoy the views across the Yorkshire Wolds.

Marton Wood

Marton

Exit junction 47 or 48 of A1(M) onto A168, signed Marton-cum-Grafton. In Marton village turn sharp right into Church Lane. Cross junction into Legram Lane, wood on left. (SE420617)
7HA (17ACRES)
North Yorkshire County Council

Nut Wood, Wauldby Scrogs & Constantine Wood ☐

Cottingham, Humberside

From Humber Bridge roundabout with the A63 head north for about 3.5km (2 miles) up A164 past a roundabout before turning left on the road to Melton. Take first turning right on the road to South Cave and follow for about 1.6km (1 mile) until road takes a long bend in front of Raywell House on the right. Opposite on left is entrance to Constantine Wood where roadside parking can normally be found.
(SE991304)
14 HA (35 ACRES)
The Woodland Trust

Woodland is a precious resource in East Yorkshire where cover has dwindled to just 1.9 per cent. But what the county lacks in quantity it makes up for in quality at Nut Wood and Wauldby Scrogs, known locally as the Bluebell Wood.

This provides a welcome oasis on a largely arable land-scape, well loved and used by local people. Parts of the woodland date from the 13th century and have a rich ground flora of dog's mercury, wood anemone, wild garlic and bluebells.

Neighbouring Constantine Wood – a baby in comparison – was created in 1999 as part of the Woodland Trust's 'Woods on your Doorstep' project, to extend and buffer the ancient woodland.

Nut Wood

In this delightful setting more than 36 bird species, 80 types of plant, 20 insect and 10 fungus species thrive – as do people, who can choose from a series of circular walks or longer walks through the site.

Little Wold Plantation

South Cave

Turn off A63 to South Cave. In South Cave turn right into Beverley Road and after 400m turn left into Little Wold Lane. Roadside parking normally available here. Little Wold Plantation can be seen on hillside and found by walking along road, which turns into bridle track before reaching wood. (SE931323)
5HA (13 ACRES)
The Woodland Trust

While little is known about the history of Little Wold Plantation, this attractive mature woodland has established itself as a favourite among walkers in the Yorkshire Wolds.

The wood can be reached from the popular Wolds Way long distance footpath which skims its southern boundary. Here, walkers can enjoy commanding views across a largely agricultural scene.

Beech and ash are dominant with a smattering of sycamore. What is striking on a tour of the woodland is the vibrant regeneration that is developing beneath the canopy of trees.

Rich in bird life, Little Wold Plantation also supports large colonies of deadly nightshade – rare in this region.

Situated on the edge of the Wolds, its elevated position offers commanding long distant views across the Vale of York from the western boundary and across the Humber estuary to North Lincolnshire when viewing to the south.

Laughton Forest

Messingham

A159 from Scunthorpe, about 5km (3 miles) south of Messingham. Access via Tuetoes Hill between Susworth and Laughton village. (SE845017)
905HA (2,237 ACRES)
Forestry Commission

Recommend a Wood

You can play a part in helping us complete this series. We are inviting readers to nominate a wood or woods they think should be included. We are interested in any woodland with public access in England, Scotland, Wales and Northern Ireland.

To recommend a wood please photocopy this page and provide as much of the following information as possible:

ABOUT THE WOOD:

   Name of wood:

   Nearest town:

   Approximate size:

   Owner/manager:

   A few words on why you think it should be included:

ABOUT YOU

   Your name:

   Your postal address:

   Post code:

If you are a member of the Woodland Trust please provide your membership number

Please send to: Exploring Woodland Guides, The Woodland Trust, Autumn Park, Dysart Road, Grantham, Lincolnshire NG31 6LL, by fax on 01476 590808 or email woodlandguides@woodland-trust.org.uk

Thank you for your help

Other Guides in the Series

If you would like to be notified when certain titles are due for publication please either write to Exploring Woodland Guides, The Woodland Trust, Autumn Park, Dysart Road, Grantham, Lincolnshire NG31 6LL or email woodlandguides@woodland-trust.org.uk

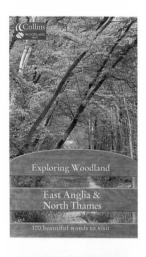

The Woodland Trust

Trees and forests are crucial to life on our planet. They generate oxygen, play host to a spectacular variety of wildlife and provide us with raw materials and shelter. They offer us tranquillity, inspire us and refresh our souls.

Founded in 1972, the Woodland Trust is now the UK's leading woodland conservation charity. By acquiring sites and campaigning for woodland it aims to conserve, restore and re-establish native woodland to its former glory. The Trust now owns and cares for over 1,100 woods throughout the UK. The Woodland Trust wants to see:

* no further loss of ancient woodland
* the variety of woodland wildlife restored and improved
* an increase in new native woodland
* an increase in people's awareness and enjoyment of woodland

The Woodland Trust has over 120,000 members who share this vision. It only costs £2.50 a month to join but your support would be of great help in ensuring the survival of Britain's magnificent heritage. For every new member, the Trust can care for approximately half an acre of native woodland. For details of how to join the Woodland Trust please either ring FREEPHONE 0800 026 9650 or visit the website at www.woodland-trust.org.uk

If you have enjoyed the woods in this book please consider leaving a legacy to the Woodland Trust. Legacies of all sizes play an invaluable role in helping the Trust to create new woodland and secure precious ancient woodland threatened by development and destruction. For further information please either call 01476 581129 or visit our dedicated website at www.legacies.org.uk

Volunteering opportunities

Would you like to help us, protect, improve and expand our precious woods? We are on the look out for new committed volunteers with a range of skills. Our volunteers do a huge range of things.

At the Woodland Trust, we value the donation of time as much as we do the donation of funds. Any work you do for us, whether it is in the woods or in the office will contribute to the Trust's key objectives. To find out more either visit our website or write, fax, give us a call or send an email.

Thank you for supporting our work.

Further Information

Public transport

Each entry gives a brief description of location, nearest town and grid reference. Traveline provides impartial journey planning information about all public transport services either by ringing 0870 608 2608 (calls charged at national rates) or visit www.traveline.org.uk. For information about the Sustrans National Cycle Network either ring 0117 929 0888 or visit www.sustrans.org.uk

Useful contacts

Forestry Commission:
www.forestry.gov.uk
tel: 0845 367 3787

National Trust:
www.nationaltrust.org.uk
tel: 0870 458 4000

Wildlife Trusts:
www.wildlifetrusts.org
tel: 0870 036 7711

RSPB:
www.rspb.org.uk
tel: 01767 680551

Royal Forestry Society:
www.rfs.org.uk
tel: 01442 822028

National Community Forest Partnership:
www.communityforest.org.uk
tel: 01684 311880

Woodland Trust:
www.woodland-trust.org.uk
tel: 01476 581111

Index

Legal & General is delighted to support the Woodland Trust's conservation programme across the UK.

As a leading UK company, Legal & General recognises the importance of maintaining and improving our environment for future generations. We actively demonstrate our commitment through good management and support of environmental initiatives and organisations, such as the Woodland Trust.

Information on how Legal & General manages its impact on the environment can be found at www.legalandgeneral.com/csr.